COACHING TEAM SHAPE
By Emilio Cecchini

and

Edizioni
Nuova
Prhomos

REEDSWAIN INC
612 Pughtown Road
Spring City, Pennsylvania 19475
1-800-331-5191
www,REEDSWAIN.COM
ISBN No.1-890946-38
Library of Congress Catalog Number 00-101756

May 1999
Copyright by Edizioni Nuova Prhomos
3, via O. Bettacchini
06012 Città di Castello (Pg), ITALY
tel. +390758550805, fax. +390758521167
Diagrams by Gregorio Camporeale
Translated by Sestilio Polimanti

Printed by Grafiche Tevere

Index

".... we are responsible for choosing
whether it is more useful for society
to form conformist minds,
able to store as much
knowledge as possible,
or if it is better to form
constructive intelligences
able to reinvent first
and then to make new inventions"

Angelo Muzzarelli

Symbols

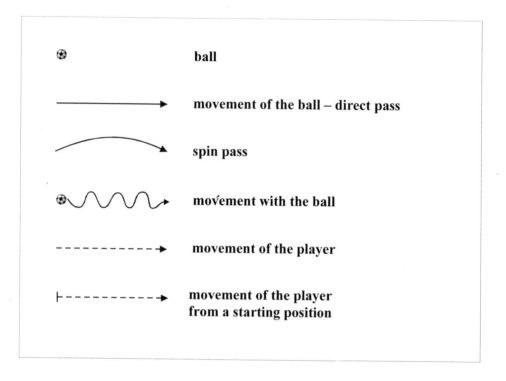

Introduction

My task is to deal with the development of tactical basic elements (prerequisites) of soccer, starting with a basic structure of three players all the way up to the whole team.

In part 1 we have seen two important concepts:

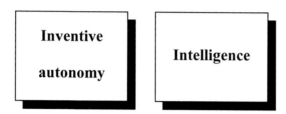

The improvement of a player depends on "coaching" his mind, his cognitive processes: inventiveness and intelligence must be enhanced. **This is the key element uniting the contents of this book**.

According to Vincenzo Prunelli, "intelligence is what results from the sum and cooperation of various skills of our mind (skills that develop thanks to environmental stimulation on our biological inheritance) and performs three *progressively nobler* tasks or fundamental functions: learning, critical assessment, inventiveness".

If learning means permanently modifying one's own behavior, from the behavior of my players and their actions (their ability to act and not only to move), I will be able to assess their achievement.

Learning will take place through use, application and coaching with "geometric" figures, appropriate methodology[1] and didactics in the 9 to 16 year old age group, taking into consideration the biological development of each individual player. Therefore, coaching should not be based on a sequence of things or exercises to carry out, but on a *"PROJECT"* whose main objective is learning.

Learning the basic elements of space in the specific context of a soccer field will be facilitated by a kind of teaching that helps every player to

---

[1] With "methodology" we refer to the systematic and assessing care taken along the way to obtain a certain result. The study of methodology is the foundation of all physical, mental and psychical disciplines (F.A., op.cit.).

understand the passages[2], instruments, functional indices and *"operations"* which are necessary to put him in a position to be aware of what he is doing, in order to learn. This kind of teaching will have to take place in a relaxed, peaceful and amusing atmosphere, where every player can move and play with his own *"inventive autonomy"* and *"creativity"* and where *"soccer is an educational instrument"* with each young player at the center of the world.

Emilio Cecchini

---

[2] The teacher we need is one who, for every "result" he wants his student to obtain, knows and can describe the operations that have made it up (F.A., op.cit).

Foreword

In "L'insegnamento dei principi d'azione tecnico-tattici nel processo di formazione calcistica giovanile - Proposta di un'organizzazione gerarchica"[3] (in "Notiziario della F.I.G.C., 4, 1996") I outlined a long-term program for the 9-12 year old age group, specifying offensive and defensive principles, basic skill elements and individual tactical intents - Scheme A. In addition, I also outlined a coaching proposal based on applied skill elements or situations of reference, using Geometric Figures to get the players to first know and then learn, the basic elements - functional tactical prerequisites - Scheme B.

The reintroduction of Geometric Figures in a specific book about tactical prerequisites is useful and consistent in consideration of the following.

The first one is about the use of Geometric Figures.

Geometric Figures are instruments which enable the young players to know and "*act*" with the distance, a point of reference, a diagonal. They already know these figures from school: by transfering them to the soccer field they can acquire, apply and improve tactical elements to be used later (skills) when, instead of "*making a movement automatic*" (doing without thinking) they will have to "*make a behavior automatic*"[4]: to think and adapt their actions to the problems they will have to face and solve in the shortest possible time.

Therefore, Geometric Figures are not "*rigid schemes*" (even if this is what the term "geometry" evokes). They are an opportunity for every young player to be free to perform experiments, learn, make mistakes, change, suggest and correct mistakes in the context of a "common principle" where the individual action is connected with the action of others[5]. Conveying this to the young players is a challenge for the coach.

This leads to the second clarification: teaching.

---

[3] "Coaching technical-tactical principles in youth soccer development process - a proposal for priority organization".

[4] This is the definition that Trapattoni prefers in high peformance soccer.

[5] A person's "operational inventiveness" ends where another person's starts, in observance of the fundamental rules of sports games, leaving the group free to express their potential (A.C., op. cit.).

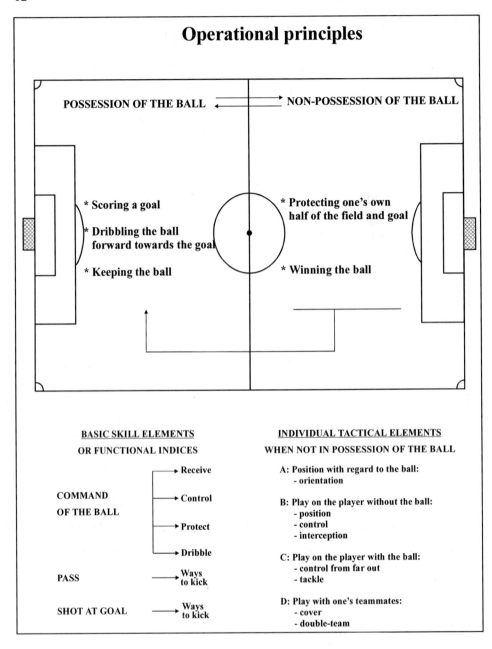

Operational principles

POSSESSION OF THE BALL ⟷ NON-POSSESSION OF THE BALL

* Scoring a goal

* Dribbling the ball
  forward towards the goal

* Keeping the ball

* Protecting one's own
  half of the field and goal

* Winning the ball

BASIC SKILL ELEMENTS	INDIVIDUAL TACTICAL ELEMENTS
OR FUNCTIONAL INDICES	WHEN NOT IN POSSESSION OF THE BALL

COMMAND
OF THE BALL
→ Receive
→ Control
→ Protect
→ Dribble

PASS → Ways to kick

SHOT AT GOAL → Ways to kick

A: Position with regard to the ball:
  - orientation

B: Play on the player without the ball:
  - position
  - control
  - interception

C: Play on the player with the ball:
  - control from far out
  - tackle

D: Play with one's teammates:
  - cover
  - double-team

Scheme A - The basic skill elements refer to the phase of possession of the ball "on offense". The individual tactical elements refer to the phase of non-possession of the ball "on defense".

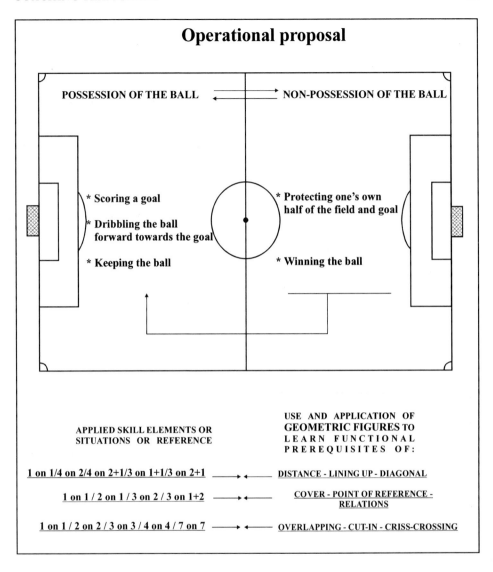

Scheme B

I agree with what Paolo Sotgiu expressed in his report on "Psycho-pedagogic Aspects of Youth Soccer Coaching" in Coverciano on June 5, 1994: *"Soccer is and must remain a game characterized by rules. It has endless educational potential thanks to the abundance and variability of its situations in which each and every member of the group has the same development opportunities. Yet it needs "LIVING DIDACTICS" and coaches who are ready to accept change"*. Living didactics must consider the contribution from scientific disciplines and go beyond the fashion in order to change and update methods and give every player the opportunity to use psycho-physical and psycho-motor skills in an adequate context. *"Living didactics is made up of continuous inspiration and inventiveness: its condition relies on contents, games and ideas really connected with youth interests, not introduced as foreign bodies"*.

Dealing with geometric figures on the soccer field can make things difficult for the coach. In fact, drawing the players' attention to exercises that do not always imply a *"rolling ball"* hinders the teaching/learning process. To partly solve this problem, in the teaching phase I suggest passing from a short theoretical explanation (visualized through sketches, figures and schemes) to the practical phase (operational phase where the players act autonomously), then going back to the theoretical phase in which the players can analyze, discuss and check with the coach if what they have done was right or wrong.

This leads to the third clarification: communication, which is a vital and essential phase in any teaching/learning process. As communication is the exchange of *"energy"* between two individuals, through those sensorial channels that connect them with the physical world *"with reciprocal influence"*, it permeates the whole teaching/learning activity and determines the accomplishment of the objectives.

It is important to take great care over the quality and ways of communication, the difficulties that might arise within this process and their psychological and behavioral side effects both on an individual and group level, and especially the methods and techniques that can be applied to improve it.

In a development context, communication should serve purposes of information, control, expression, social contact and stimulation in a relaxed atmosphere of wellbeing and in a multidirectional way: from coach to players, from players to coach, from players to players. Players and coach are not on two different sides of a fence: they are together and any thought, reflection, consideration and question leads to learning.

"The coach stops being a trainer to become the one who stimulates to action, without pushing the team's determination to excess: he is the director of a concerted and very complex process that goes beyond the world of soccer. In other words, he is an EXPERT IN HUMAN DEVELOPMENT helping each individual player to achieve maximum results without ever setting aside the native potential they are endowed with", (P.S:, op. cit.).

Finally, the fourth clarification: because today I can talk of a *"project"*.
A project is made up of the consideration of environmental conditions, analysis of available spaces and resources, and especially skills and potential of the group of players (R.B., op.cit.). It is the operational response to an educational problem: in our case, building, defining and giving concrete form to methods and operational sequences through the use and application of geometric figures in order to produce learning.

From my personal and my colleagues' experience, I have seen that this method[6], if applied with the suggested details, gives good results, reduces learning time, consolidates the player's personality and favors the development of everybody's potential.

And now... let's take the field.

---

[6] This method is definitely successful not only for tactical behavior or automatic acquisition of available space, but also as a real form of motor development with ensuing availability to carry out coordinated movements in a group context (A.C., op. cit. 1990).

Chapter 1

BASIC TEACHING SEQUENCES: LEARNING THE CONCEPT OF DISTANCE AND LINING UP

- ❑ Learning the concept of distance
- ❑ Learning the concept of lining up
- ❑ "Acting", playing with the concepts of distance and lining up

Learning the Concept of Distance

The players are divided into groups of three. The exercises usually start from the goal line.

❑ **Phase A**

Mark with cones (or small flags) three positions at equal distance from one another[7]. Three players are arranged as shown on diagram 1A: they must solve the following "*problem*":
"*You must reach the end of the field while jogging and keeping starting distances unchanged*"[8].
Then all the other groups do the same.
This first phase is made easier by the presence of cones (or small flags) along the circuit. These help the young players to visualize the circuit and keep the initial distances.
At the end of each leg the young players change positions.

❑ **Phase B**

After some repetitions and careful observation, the young players are asked to discuss with the coach what they have been doing. The coach asks questions like "*How did you do to ...?*", "*What difficulties have you run into when...?*", "*What could we do in order to...?*", "*How could we change...?*", "*What is the meaning of what we are doing?*", "*Why are we doing this?*", etc.
That is, the coach asks the young players to talk, describe and comment on the movements they have made, teaching them to reflect upon what they have learned.

Discussing the activity carried out facilitates and improves learning.

---

[7] At first, distances range from 3 to 6 yards, then they are increased. Experience shows that young players find it easier to play on short distances.
[8] One half of the field is the minimum space required by this kind of exercise. Of course, there could be problems if there are teams of other age groups practicing at the same time in the same field; I have often had to settle for one quarter of the field when men's teams were training too. This is not an ideal "*environment*" to carry out the coaching as the young players watch the adults and as a consequence lose concentration.

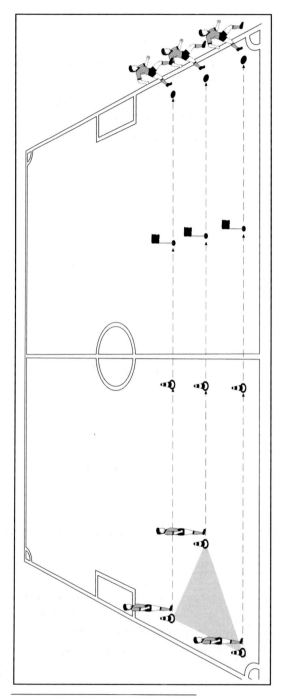

Diagram 1A[1]

---

[1] The diagrams with soccer fields do not show all the lines in order to make the diagrams clearer and facilitate immediate understanding of the activity.

❏ **Phase C**

After the young players have performed the first repetitions, the drill goes on with more elements and markers. For example, as they are jogging from one end of the field to the other the coach signals them to carry out movements established beforehand: jumping, bending, sitting down on the ground, diving into a prone position, somersaulting[10], turning around, making a 360-degree turn, etc., as shown in diagram 1B.

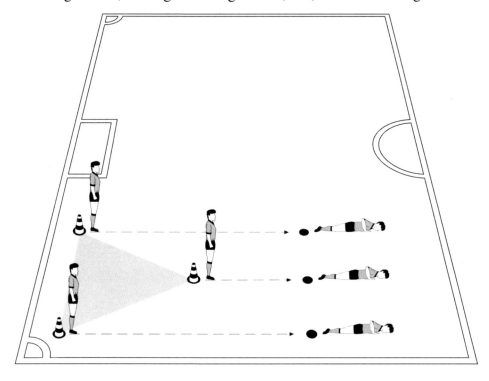

Diagram 1B - The three young players dive into a prone position when the coach gives the signal.

Phase D

This is a competitive phase in which the young players "*act*" together (in one half of the field 15-18 players can be adquately coached).

> *"Acting" is a process regulated by the objective, the process, the result.*
> *(W. B., Op. cit.)*

---

[10] Of course, the coach should make sure beforehand that the young players can somersault, so as to avoid possible injuries. Hand support on the ground is compulsory.

Suggestion:
"Which group will reach the goal line first, while keeping initial distances unchanged?"
Some of the conditions of Phase C can be applied.
The exercise can be made more lively and motivating by giving each group the name of an animal or the name of a cartoon character.

❑ **Phase E**
A ball certainly motivates and stimulates a young player.
During the early coaching period control and dribble might not be adequate and so keeping the initial distance along the circuit could become quite hard: however, the objective will be accomplished later on, once control and dribble have evolved and become adequate. With a ball, both learning the concept of distance and basic skills can be improved.
Effective coaching starts when individual players face their limitations and make mistakes: then they need a coach, a *"teacher"*, a *"didactic advisor"*, a *"guide"* and not a *"person who knows more than they do"*.

❑ **Phase F**
From perception to representation: the starting distances must be kept unchanged without any points of reference. This is the last phase of comparative teaching.

Table A is a summary of the six phases:

OPERATIONAL-APPLICATION PHASES OF EVERY EXERCISE	
PHASE	**DISTINCTIVE ELEMENTS**
A	❏ Explanation and objective of the exercise - "*acting*"
B	❏ Communication: talking together, interacting, assessing the activity
C	❏ Back to "*action*" (then, addition of motor skill movements)
D	❏ Competition - contest
E	❏ Use of the ball
F	❏ From perception to representation

Table A

Some points abouts the conditions of the coaching phases should be underlined.

1. Considering that the 9-12 year old age group spends on average 90 minutes in the field, this kind of coaching divided into phases can be carried out for 15-20 minutes a session, which can be also subdivided in two periods.

   It is hard to place it at the beginning of the session: as they take the field the young players need to move, run, play and spend their energy. I think the first of the two periods should be placed in the central phase of the session, and the second one towards the end.

   Sometimes, depending on the invidual personalities in the group, it can be better to place this kind of coaching at the beginning, with a length determined by the "*active, aware and motivated participation*" of the group.

2. It is never too early to suggest rules and regulations (the so-called "*phases of guided play/coaching/unrestricted play*")[11]

> **Getting the players consciously used to rules.**

---

[11]I do not mean to minimize the importance of the match as a coaching instrument, but I think that leaving the players free to play without restrictions is not fruitful.

3. I have no answer to the question: *"How long do the young players take to consolidate in their motor skills what the coach is trying to teach them?"*. In every developmental process, a new acquisition is possible only if it is supported by an adequate level of maturation enabling the performance of certain "actions".

    The coach must consider this fundamental factor of maturation (*"the inner activity determining the subsequent steps of the child's development"*): certain actions will show only at a certain point of the child's development, not before, therefore they cannot be learned at a time which is not consistent with their level of maturity.

4. A joyful, tranquil and friendly atmosphere is extremely important.

5. Is it too much to ask for adequate equipment, a sufficient number of new balls, availability of the field (if possible, with grass)?

Table B is a summary of the didactic process referring to the method applied:

COACH	PLAYER
❑ Get the players involved, set common objectives, assess the results together	❑ Understand the aim of the exercises, movements, actions
❑ Make all the players aware of the teaching and learning process	❑ Attribute the right meaning to each point of reference or signal
❑ Inform the players about difficulties; give adequate advice	❑ Listen to the coach's advice
❑ Carefully watch the performance of each player	❑ Reflect on your performance
❑ Accept the players' ideas, points of view, incitements	❑ Always be motivated in order to understand, learn and improve
❑ Stimulate communication and cooperation	❑ Communicate with individual teammates and the group
❑ Allow the necessary time to practice, reflect and learn	❑ Be a member and feel like a member of a group
❑ Create a joyful, tranquil and friendly atmosphere	
❑ Be a *"facilitator of learning"*	

Table B - Didactic processes and performances expected of the player.

Learning the Concept of Lining Up

In the same way as before, the young players are still divided into groups of three and required to jog forward while keeping both the starting distance and the lining up (being along the same line and not in front or behind the others)[12] unchanged. They need to get to the midfield line all together at the same time, as shown in diagram 2:

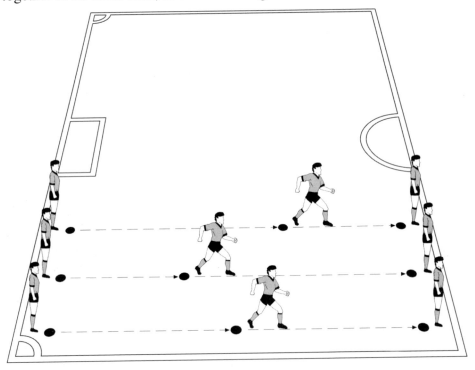

Diagram 2 - The performance of the three players in the middle is wrong, while the one of those on the right (midfield) is correct.

To perform the exercise correctly, the young players should watch each other, communicate and run at equal speed, which is not easy at first as it requires them to reflect.

The objective is accomplished by repeating the exercise and making the players change positions to make them get accurate visual perception from different points.

---

[12] In order to help the young players immediately understand what they need to do, they can be positioned either side by side with their arms outstretched or along one line of the field.

Of course it is more difficult when coaching the lining up with four or more players.

"Acting" and Playing with the Concepts of Distance and Lining Up

The so-called *"Game of the Cities"*, derived from the Dutch school (Tesi Matulli, op.cit.), combines an understanding of the first space elements with the practice of more complex geometric figures.

The space needed is a square (see diagram 3) at whose corners four 8-yard squares are marked and given the names of cities (or countries, parts of the town, etc.)[13]. The exercise below is carried out by 20 young players, each with a ball, divided into four 5-player teams with shirts of a different color.

❑ **First phase**

The young players are in the middle of the field, carrying out whichever technical movement they like. When the coach gives the signal each team must dribble the ball to their pre-established "city-square".

This phase can be suitable to practice cooperation and communication if we require all five players of each team to enter their city at the same time.

> *"Watching, acting, communicating and cooperating with others".*

❑ **Second phase**

Without restrictions, the young players dribble the ball across the *"roads"* and cross all the cities to go back to the one they started from. *"Traffic lights"* can be added to make this movement livelier: when the coach calls out *"green"* the players should run, *"yellow"* they should slow down, *"red"* they should stop (stop the ball); or else, different meanings can be given to a certain number of whistles (one, two, three) or to signals given with the fingers.

Also a competition among the teams can be motivating: the winner is the first team to reach their town.

---

[13] This structure is very helpful to develop the sense of play and control of the ball in 6/7year-old players.

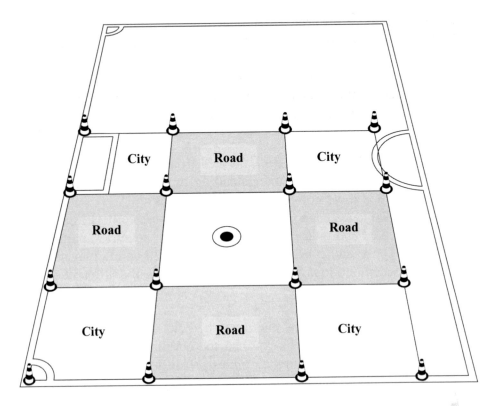

Diagram 3 - The size of the field shown is bigger than that of the space where the game is played to help immediate understanding.

❏ **Third phase**

Three young players are placed at equal distance from each other (diagram 4).

They slowly cross the four cities without the ball while keeping their distances and positions (A inside, B in the middle, C outside) unchanged. The exercise is then carried out by all the others.

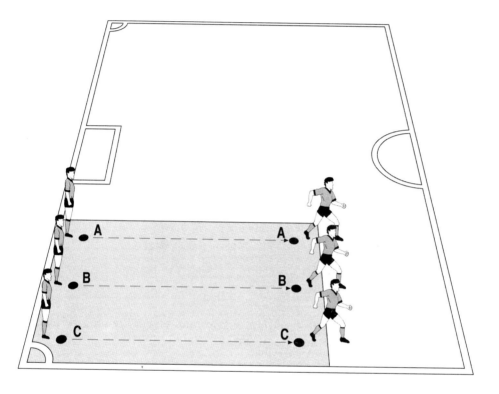

Diagram 4 - The "*city*" and the distances shown are bigger to favor immediate understanding.

❑ **Fourth phase**
A fourth young player (D) is added to the group: he is placed in front, to represent the top of a triangle made up by A, B, C and D (diagram 5).

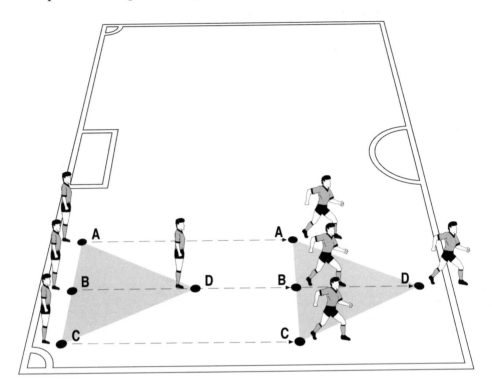

Diagram 5

The players carry out the same exercise as before, but in this case cooperation and communication are more targeted and intense (for instance, D must also look back, B must suggest distances, etc.).

❏ **Fifth phase**

A fifth young player (E) is added behind the group, as distant from B as B is from D (diagram 6), so as to form a figure that the players immediately recognize as a diamond or a kite[14].

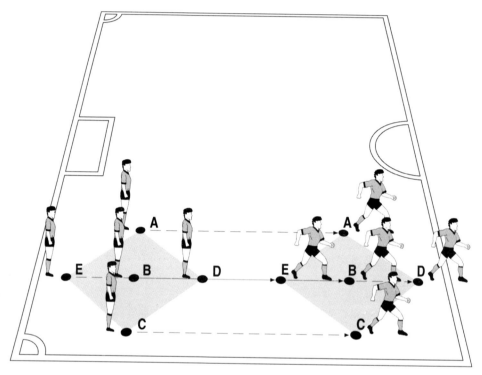

Diagram 6

The players carry out the same movement as in the third phase: first without the ball, then with the ball and changing their starting positions.

This exercise should be carried out in different sessions as it is an opportunity for coaching both the contents related to the pre-established objective and many others.

It gets the players involved and determines a *"joyful racket"* with calls and shouts aiming at stimulating, slowing down, "acting".

The proposed exercises are tiring but they are also amusing, their atmosphere is relaxed and they improve learning how to move in the field.

---

[14] The diamond and the kite are fundamental figures, dealt with in specific paragraphs.

Chapter 2

A THREE-PLAYER STRUCTURE

❑ The triangle
❑ Combinations of triangles in a row
❑ Combinations of triangles in a line

The triangle

The geometric figure we are going to consider is the triangle, a structure[15] made up of three elements.

❑ **Sequence A**

Let's draw on the ground a 5 to 9-yard equilateral triangle[16] by using plastic tape and three cones (diagram 7, top left corner).

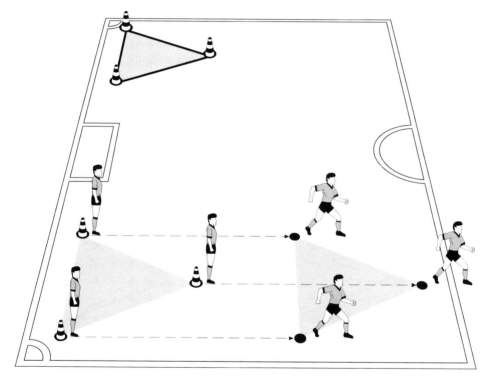

Diagram 7

---

[15] With "structure" we also mean "figure", "system", "arrangement".

[16] This is the easiest figure to "*assimilate*" as its corners and sides are equal. Later on other kinds of triangle will also be used.

❏ **Sequence B**

Three players are placed on the angles of the triangle in the direction shown in diagram 7 (bottom left corner).

When the coach gives the signal the players jog in a rectilinear direction towards the midfield or goal line *"while keeping the initial distance"*.

Then, they walk back to the starting point as they like.

As we said, all the exercises must be carried out in a different position at each leg, so in this case the players take turns on the three angles.

Diagram 8A shows what to do if the players find it difficult to maintain the initial figure: tie the three players around their hips with plastic tape for a length equal to the side of the triangle, so that in order to keep the tape tight the three players are forced to maintain the distance during the exercise.

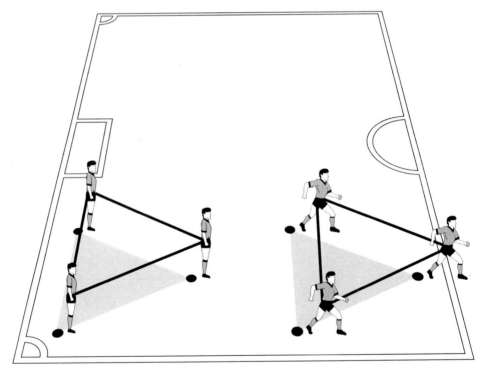

Diagram 8A

The plastic tape helps the players to maintain the right distance, besides it can be fun when they use it for *"pulling"*, *"tying"*, *"loosening"*, *"tightening"*, etc.

> ### *Plastic tape for playing and learning*

Another problem could be the difficulty in maintaining a rectilinear direction. Cones, pins, small flags or balls can be placed along the circuit to help (diagram 8B).

Diagram 8B

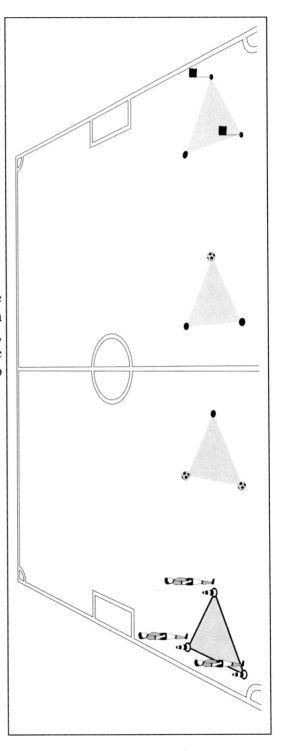

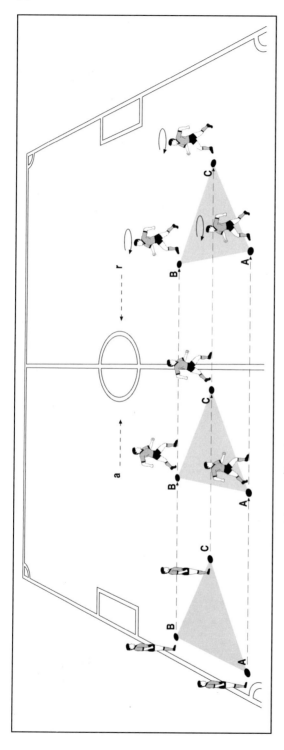

□ **Sequence C**

When the coach gives the signal, the players move forward from the starting triangle: first they walk, then they start jogging slightly increasing their speed up to 40 or 50 percent of their maximum.

When the coach gives another pre-established signal (whistle, handclap, etc.) the players turn around and return to their starting position at the same speed while keeping distances unchanged, so as to reach the angles of the figure at the same time (diagram 9).

This is difficult for the players, because at the same time they must consider the arrival point and keep the same speed in order to maintain the distances (*psychokinetic principle*).

Diagram 9

During movement "**a**", players A and B control both the distance between them and from player C: they suggest possible variations and adjustments to maintain the initial figure.

When they return (movement "**r**") player C suggests possible variations and adjustments: he directs, stimulates, gives orders and adapts the run and the positions of his teammates to his own.

In a match there are many situations in which, from behind, a player directs or calls his teammates, calls movements, pressure, cover etc. ("*tactical communication*").

During the drills without the ball, we usually introduce the elements shown in table C to motivate the players and get better concentration.

EXERCISES WITHOUT THE BALL

❑   Vary the kind of movement in a leg
❑   Vary speed
❑   Vary conditions
❑   Combine various motor skills
❑   Vary the ways of receiving stimulation and information

Table C

Sequence D

The exercise continues as shown in diagram 10: with three cones
marking a triangle (2) near the triangle made up of plastic tape and
cones (1). In this way the players have only one point of reference (the
cones). Then, the exercise is carried out with the players acting as
points of reference (3) (*"representation of the geometric figure"*).

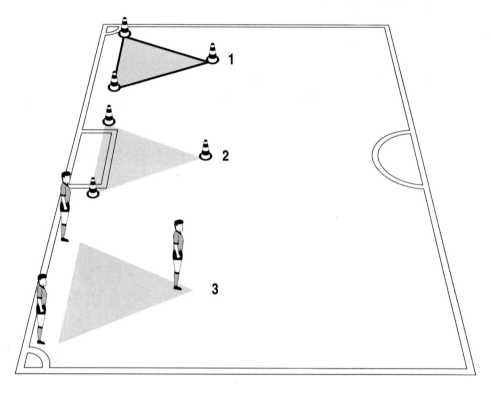

Diagram 10

At this point *Phase B* is introduced: discussion and points of view, together
with assessment of the activity carried out. Any doubts and hesitations must
be addressed by listening to all that the players tell the coach.

The ball is present all through the coaching session.	Then, once the coach is satisfied that the players have learned the objectives of ***Phase B***, he can introduce the ball and go on to ***Phase C***.

Table D shows how the coaching phases with the ball must be carried out and varied.

EXERCISES WITH THE BALL

- ❑ Vary the ways of dribbling
- ❑ Vary the speed of dribbling
- ❑ Vary the movements
- ❑ Combine skills and physical exercises
- ❑ Vary the direction of dribbling
- ❑ Vary the ways of receiving stimulation and information

Table D

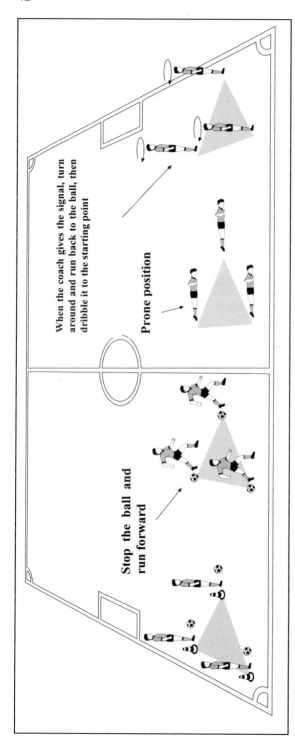

☐ **Exercise 1**

Because this exercise includes all the suggested phases, it is a valuable way to end this first part of the activity.

It requires a high degree of concentration and illustrates the numerous operational sequences that this kind of method can offer[17] (see diagram 11).

Diagram 11

[17] Distances and direction must be maintained unchanged all through the exercise.

❏ **Exercise 2**

This exercise draws on the "*Game of the Cities*" exercise but is more difficult.

The players (15 to 18 at the same time) are arranged in a triangle and must change positions at the top of the triangle at every change of direction (diagram 12).

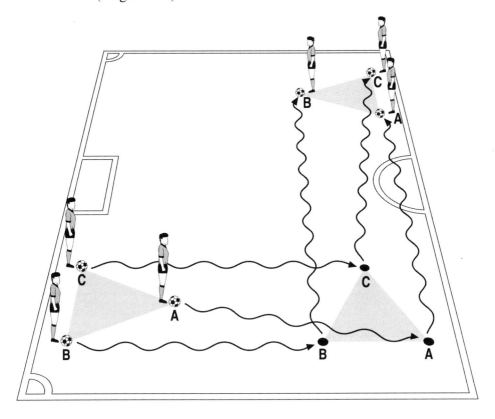

Diagram 12

After verifying that the players respond correctly and work without difficulty with spacial elements, we can now introduce exercises that transfer the above concepts to a soccer context, **which is the main objective of this method**.

This method is functional and useful as each geometrical exercise "contains and develops" soccer situations.

❑ **Exercise 3**

Players A, B and C are arranged in a right-angled triangle (diagram 13).
A has the ball, passes it to C then runs to position A_1, overlapping C.
After receiving the ball, C passes it to B who passes it on to A_1 and
then moves forward to position B_1, by C and along the same line in
order to rebuild the starting figure.
A_1 passes the ball to C who immediately restarts the exercise up to the
goal line.

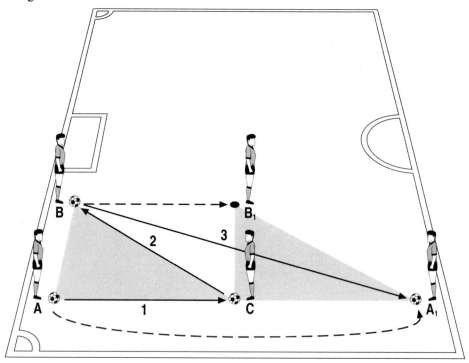

Diagram 13 - "*Overlapping*" is the aim of this exercise.

The players must maintain the starting figure (the right-angled triangle
in this case) all through the length of the movement while carrying out
basic technical movements.
Then, the players change their starting positions in order to visualize
the different visual angles that the movements involve.
The exercise is carried out on both sides of the field.

❑ **Exercise 4**

This exercise is similar to the previous one, but the direction of the movement differs as shown in diagram 14 (right-to-left diagonal of the field).

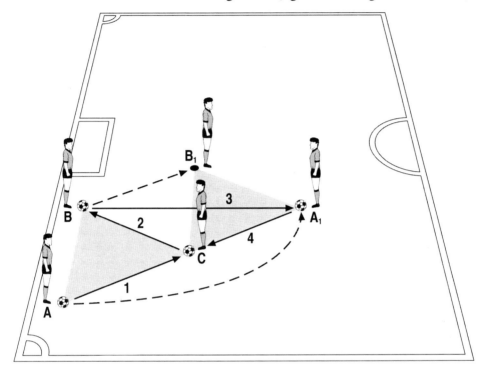

Diagram 14

In this exercise as well the players change their starting positions, maintain the starting figure (equilateral triangle) and carry out technical and tactical movements.

The exercises carried out along the left-to-right and right-to-left diagonals provide the players with a lot of visual angles and fronts of direction, and, in time, will teach them to naturally become aware of their orientation in their zone of the field during the game.

❏ **Exercise 5**

This exercise contains several soccer movements: *"overlapping"*, *"cut-in"*, *"support"*.

The players are positioned as shown in diagram 15: C has the ball and passes it to B, then moves backward to position C_1.

Player B passes to A and overlaps to position B_1. A passes to C_1 and cuts-in to position A_1 along the same line as B_1 and so on. Positions C_1, B_1 and C_1 redraw the starting triangle.

When carried out in the center of the field, this exercise can finish with a shot at goal.

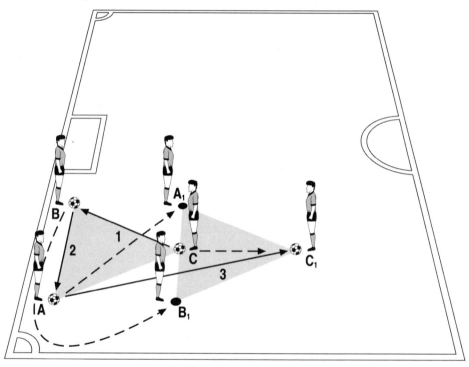

Diagram 15

❑ **Exercise 6**

Like the previous exercise, this one also contains several soccer movements (*"support"*, *"cut-in"*).

The players are placed as shown in diagram 16: B passes to C and runs to position B_1 (he carries out movements to change the front of the action); C passes to A and moves to position C_1 (movements to widen and change the front of the action); A passes to B_1 and moves to position A_1 (along the same line as C_1 in order to maintain the initial distance and make himself available for support).

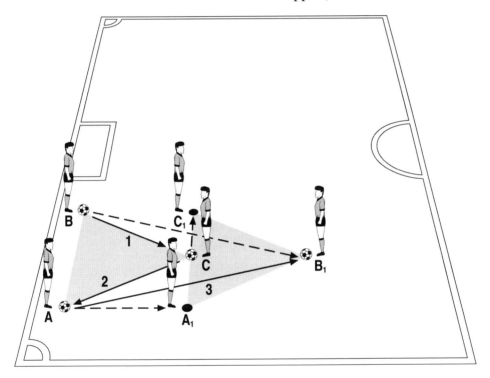

Diagram 16

Combinations of Triangles in a Row

The following exercises involve a considerable number of players in solving one problem[18].

---

[18] The phases shown in Table A are applied.

❑ **Exercise 7**

In this exercise (diagram 17) 12 players are divided in 4 three-player groups. Each group forms a triangle and moves forward and backward while carrying out pre-established movements and conforming to one another at the same time. That is, each player is a member of his triangle-structure and, at the same time, also a member of the overall structure formed by the four triangles.

Moving along the same LM and PQ line involves 8 and 4 players respectively at the same time.

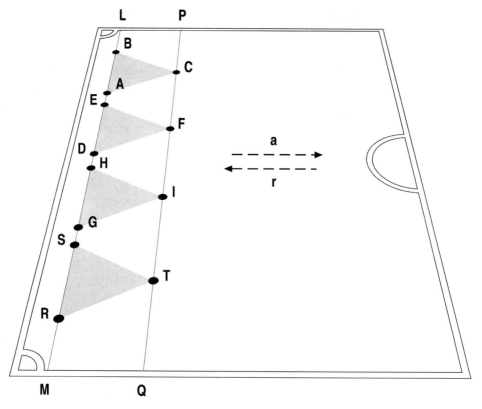

Diagram 17

With these exercises the players reinforce communication and cooperation, understanding that they are all a part of one group sharing a common objective.

┌─────────────────────────┐
│ *In today's soccer*   │
│ *perception is vital.* │
└─────────────────────────┘

Besides, they are coached to have better vision, see more elements, see further and make themselves available for the ball.

The outside players, in our example A - B and R - S, must conform their movements both to those of their teammates inside and in front. D - E - G - H watch their teammates on the left, on the right and in front, to keep the whole structure under control. The same applies to C - F - I - T on the way back ("r").

Diagram 18 shows a further combination of triangles in a row arranged along three lines which involves 15 players.

From the geometrical point of view the aims of this exercise are the same as in the previous one.

From the soccer point of view, this exercise shows three horizontal lines with the following meaning:

X - Y line: first line: attack line
P - Q line: second line: midfield line
L - M line: third line: defense line

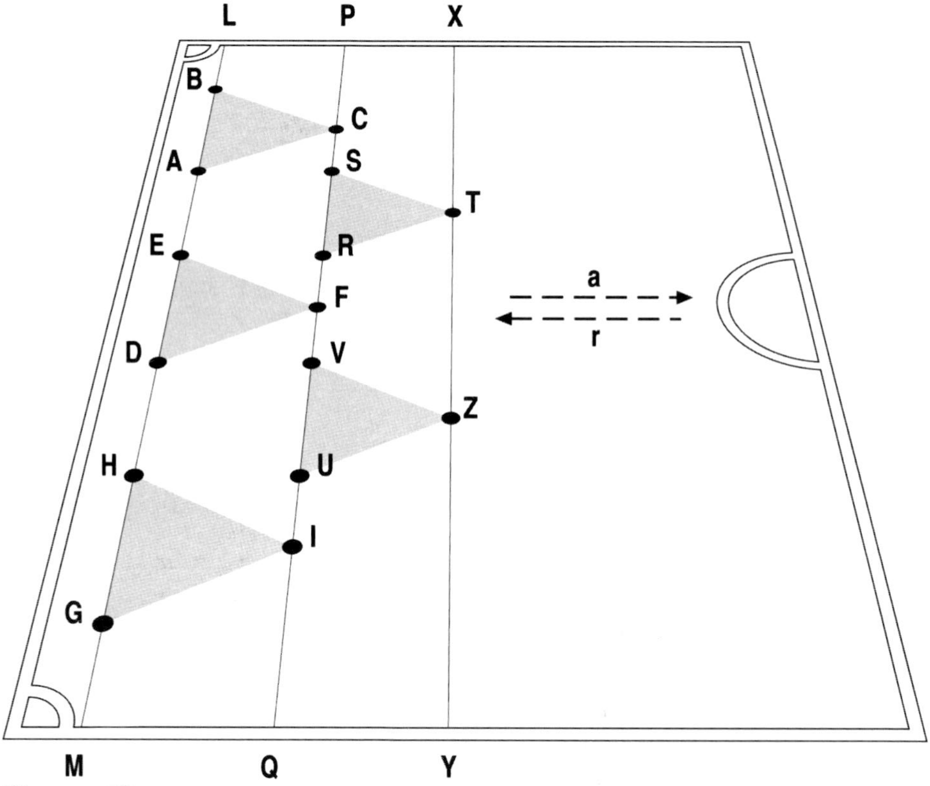

Diagram 18

The exercise can also be carried out as follows: players R - S and U -V are placed along the X - Y line, while T and Z are placed along the P - Q line, so as to have 4 players along the first line and 5 along the second.
This structure offers many coaching opportunities.

❑ *Suggestion*

When the coach gives the signal all the players start jogging slowly while dribbling the ball. When the coach whistles, B - D - E - G - S - F - U increase their speed and go beyond the lines; when the coach whistles again everybody stops. Diagram 19 shows the resulting figure.

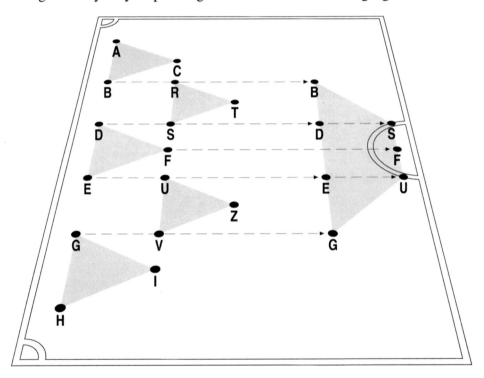

Diagram 19 - Only the final figure has been drawn.

Combinations of Triangles in a Line

9 players are arranged in three triangular structures as shown in diagram 20. This exercise is carried out and has the same objectives as those seen up to now. It contains new geometric and soccer concepts.

The most striking one is the "*diagonal*", the dotted line connecting B - C - D and A - C - E (we have drawn only two in order to make the drawing clearer).

Each player, except I, must form and maintain the diagonal all through the movements indicated by the arrows (a) and (r).

Another concept is contained in the position of players C - F: they are connected with A - B - D - E and D - E - G - H respectively. They have the role of "*points of reference*", "*links*" for the teammates behind and in front of them.

We can see also the rhombus/diamond made by F - H - I - G, which in soccer is usually defined as a "*box*". The players in this position have an important role, since this figure (changeable in its geometric aspects - angles, distance) must maintain positional connections in order to be functional during the game.

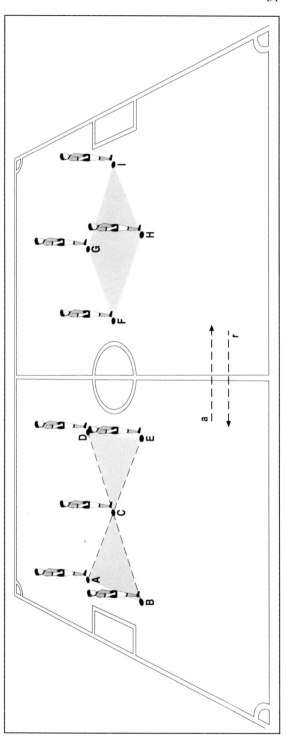

Diagram 20

The combinations of triangles in a row and in a line we have shown so far can be used in the daily coaching program. They are usually placed in the warm-up and active recovery phases, both with 11 to 12 year olds and 13 to 14 year olds.

❑ *Suggestion*

With the players moving, when the coach gives the signal the players stop and pass the ball to each other at 2 to 3 touches (at one touch if they have the necessary skills). Or else, he can coach a 2 on 1 exercise focused on maintaining ball possession (using the triangle, if possible).

Chapter 3

A FOUR-PLAYER STRUCTURE

❏   The diamond/rhombus - kite

The Diamond/Rhombus - Kite

Given the importance of this arrangement in today's soccer I have divided the teaching sequence in **3 phases**, first with geometric and then soccer exercises.

Phase 1 **Geometric movement of the rhombus, considering the C - A line joining the center of the goal**

The four players A - B - C - D start from the central position (diagram 21) and get their bearings from points P and Q (marked with small flags or balls). During their movements they maintain the geometric characteristics of their figure, having as a point of reference the line by which P and Q join the center of the goal.

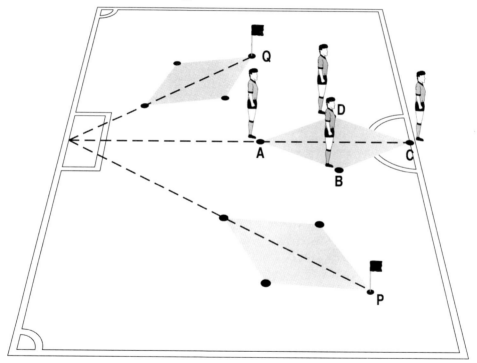

Diagram 21

In order to make the exercise easier, especially at first, a plastic tape can be used for two purposes. First, to mark the line joining P and Q and the center of the goal, and, second, to be held by the four players to make their movement uniform, helping to maintain the distances and angles between them.

Phase 2 **Movement of the rhombus, considering player A as a pivot and taking away the plastic tape joining P and Q and the center of the goal**

The four players A - B - C - D have the two points of reference P and Q but A does not move, as he acts as a pivot. Diagram 22 shows two transformations (top and bottom box) obtained by the three players by changing their distances, angles and movement direction: this enables them to learn the connections among all the elements involved in the structure.

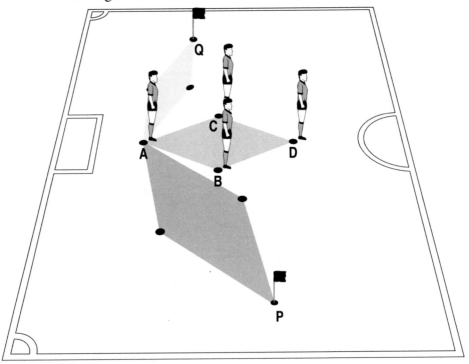

Diagram 22

Phase 3   Movement of the rhombus in a soccer situation

The four players start form the the basic position and, as shown in diagram 23, they move towards player P (who has the ball), keeping in mind the line joining the ball and the center of the goal. The closest player to the ball, B, goes towards it (position B_1) and determines the movement of his three teammates.

The movement of D - C - A is important: they go to positions D_1 - C_1 - A_1 and maintain the figure while varying their connections[19].

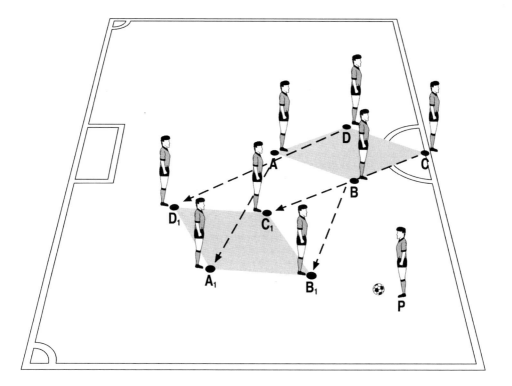

Diagram 23

---

[19] Diagram 23 shows two regular rhombuses, but in this phase the geometrical features do not need to be respected; therefore angles and distance can vary.

The exercise shows how player B determines the action ("*common intention*") of his three teammates in order to keep a constant balance all through the defensive phase.

During the play, especially with more opponents, the movements of A – C - D are adapted in the most functional way.

> ***The rhombus is only a point of reference, a figure: yet, it gives the players the "key" to solve the ever-changing "situation" of play.***

During the coaching it is vital to consider connections and the principle of mutual movements.

Experience shows that coaching soccer concepts through this figure takes a long time.

The coach should start from static situations (at first also using plastic tape) and then move on to dynamic ones, changing the points of reference and making the players take turns in the different positions and tasks of the structure.

In every exercise it is very important to make a player start from different visual angles. The objective is to improve perception.

The ball should always be used, with the dual functions as a signal and as a point of reference. This develops the action.

I recommend a combination of forward movement of the rhombus with technical-tactical elements.

The players are arranged as shown in diagram 24: C has the ball, passes it to A and then overlaps B, getting to position C_1 at a distance of 4 to 5 yards from A.

As soon as they are passed by player C, players B and D run forward to reach positions B_1 and D_1 respectively. After receiving the ball from C, A turns around and passes to C_1, and then runs to position A_1 overlapping B_1, thus again forming the starting rhombus.

The exercise continues up to the goal line.

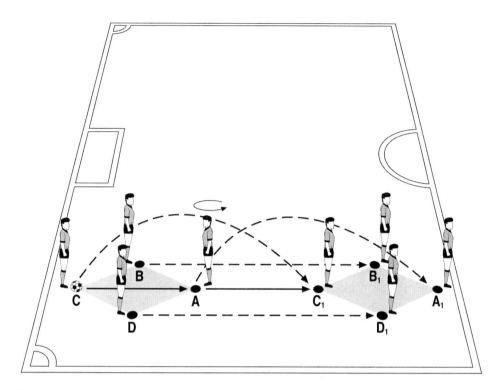

Diagram 24

The coaching method suggested with the *"rhombus"* is especially useful for coaching the 10 year olds, who are already familiar with this figure as they practiced the *"kite"* in previous age groups. With the 7-8 year olds, in the numerous matches 5 against 5 (or 4 against 4, without the goalkeeper), we place the four moving players in a kite-shaped arrangement and each position has the following meaning:

> *"Role" is only a term: our young players play all roles.*

- tail of the kite (near the goal): central defender;
- right angle of the kite: right midfielder;
- left angle of the kite: left midfielder;
- head of the kite: central attacker.

4 against 4[20] is the minimum number of players that are needed to have a successful exercise without loss of the ingredients of soccer:

- ball;
- teammates;
- opponents;
- space;
- direction;
- rules;
- time;
- competition and tension.

These small sided matches can help develop all technical, motor, physical and intellectual skills and potential, sense of play and relationships. The number of players makes it possible to play forward, wide or backward, in match-like situations which the young players can easily recognize, choosing the best option in terms of control and speed of the ball, direction of the pass, attack and defense.

I think that with players of the age groups we have mentioned, it is very useful to alternate phases of play/fun (such as the 4 against 4 match on a 20 x 30 yard area) with geometric figure teaching (for a short time).

This requires the passion, involvement, enthusiasm, competence and perseverance of the coach, often in a difficult, unstable and indifferent environment[21], but if we want to "*educate*" our players to the principles discussed above, the introduction of this method in the "*Soccer School*" programs can only improve their performance, achieving good results.

> *At a youth level the result is important..., but only to some extent.*

Result to be considered only as a final objective.

---

[20] Introduced as a symbol of the Dutch Method in 1986.

[21] As many of my former students can confirm.

Chapter 4

A FIVE-PLAYER STRUCTURE

❏   Lining-up and diagonals

Lining-up and diagonals

❑ **Lining-up: movement of B and D along the horizontal line formed by A - C – E**

Five players are arranged as shown in diagram 25: C is part of two triangles (D - C - E and C - B - A) and must act as a point of reference for his moving teammates A - B - D - E.

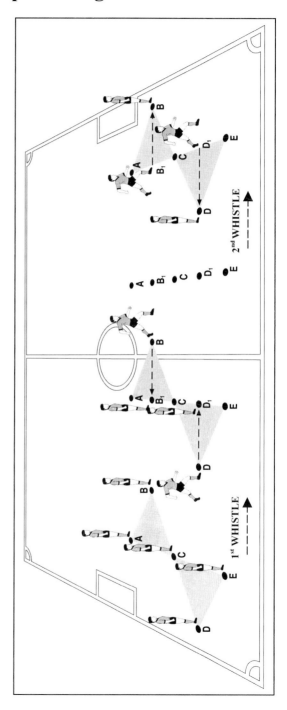

Diagram 25 - Some players have not been drawn in order to make the diagram clearer.

When the coach gives the signal, the five players move forward along the field. On the first whistle, B and D, while moving, go to positions B_1 (between A and C, by running backward) and D_1 (between C and E, by running forward) respectively, so as to be along the same line as A - C - E.

On the second whistle, keeping the same pace and direction, B and D rebuild the starting structure with a reverse movement. A - C - E must facilitate the exercise by giving advice to their teammates and by making their pace uniform. All five players are involved in the successful performance of this exercise, with each successfully performing a specific function. They must get used to cooperation and "*mutual help*", playing together and for each other.

The exercise is first carried out slowly and without the ball, then increasingly faster and with the ball.

❑ **Diagonal: movement of A - E to the same line as B - C - D**

The players are arranged as shown in diagram 26. When the coach gives the signal, the 5 players move forward. On the first whistle, A and E (while moving) build a diagonal with their teammates B - C - D. A moves forward-sideways to the right and E moves backward-sideways to the left.

They continue to move forward in this diagonal arrangement. On a second whistle by the coach, A and E rebuild the starting structure with a reverse movement.

Once the players perform the movements correctly and have understood their meaning with regard to the pre-established objectives, they can move on to a more complex exercise: alternation of diagonals and lining-ups during the forward movement. They start from the positions we have already described.

When the coach gives the signal they build the diagonal.

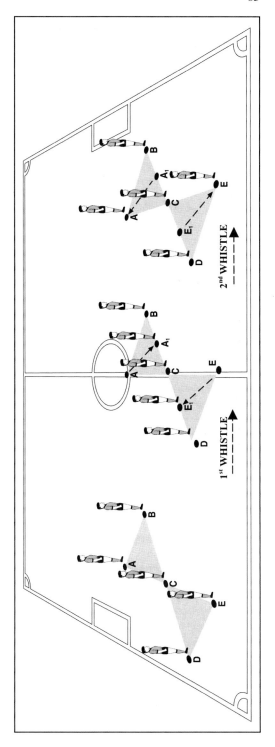

Diagram 26

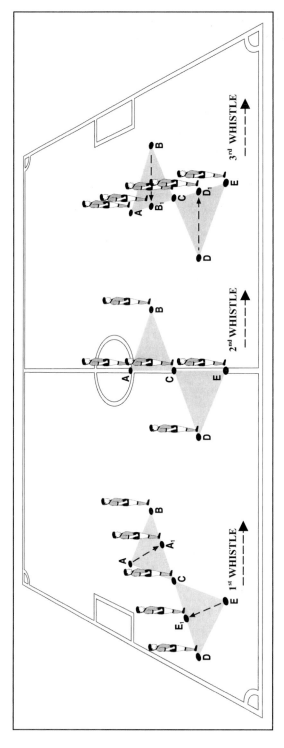

Then, they rebuild the starting figure (basic position) and, when the coach gives a further signal, they carry out movements in order to be lined up (diagram 27).

Diagram 27

In order to develop the players' concentration, a certain signal (a handclap for instance) should correspond to the diagonal, while another one (a whistle) to the lining-up.

These exercises are usually carried out by 11 year olds but they can be introduced in earlier age groups if the players are receptive.

The difficulty of these exercises lies in their "*totality*": the 5 players are not separate elements, they are a group whose teamwork is superior to the sum of the actions of the individual players ("*the principle of totality must be the basis of coaching*", P. S. - F. P., op. cit.). Each player must perform his task and at the same time coordinate his action with that of his teammates.

The difficulty of the exercise is also determined by the number of players involved, the space to be covered, the signals, the attention required to be paid to the coach's and the teammates' instructions. These difficulties can be overcome by drawing the movements, using coaching aids, walking while carrying out the first movements and ... with a lot of patience.

Chapter 5

A SIX-PLAYER STRUCTURE

❑   Exercises with various figures

Exercises with various figures

Form a 16-yard equilateral triangle with three cones.
As shown in diagram 28, place 3 players at its corners and 3 in the middle of each side so that two triangles are formed, one by A - B - C and one by D - E - F. Let's not consider at this point the other geometric figures that have been formed.

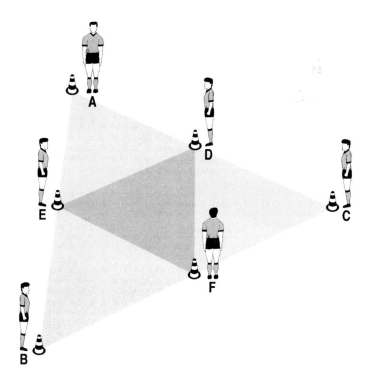

Diagram 28

❑ **Exercise 1**

Each player has a ball and carries out control exercises. When the coach gives the signal the 6 players dribble the ball clockwise or counterclockwise (counterclockwise in diagram 29).

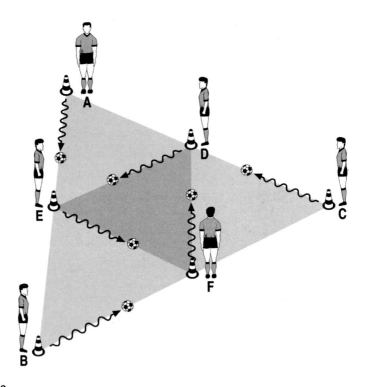

Diagram 29

A - B - C dribble the ball along the bigger triangle, turning around its corners; D - E - F along the smaller, changing direction when they get to the middle of the sides of the bigger triangle. If we synchronize their pace, D - E - F cover the smaller triangle twice while A - B - C cover the bigger one.

■ *Objectives:*
1. maintaining the distances;
2. improving peripheral vision;
3. improving kinesthetic sense (conforming one's pace to the teammates' - connection with psychokinetics);
4. improving specific skills.

❑ **Exercise 2**

The players are arranged as in diagram 30; each of them has a ball and carries out control exercises.

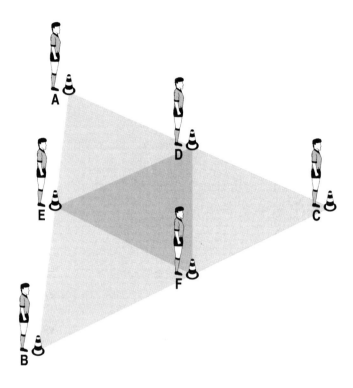

Diagram 30

When the coach gives the signal, A and B dribble the ball forward and get to positions A_1 and B_1 on C's sides and on the prolongation of diagonals E - D and E - F (see diagram 31).

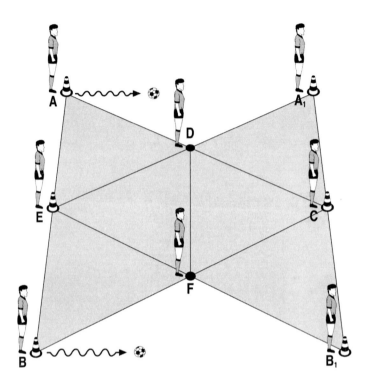

Diagram 31

In this way the figure is flipped: player E is the point of reference behind.

- ***Soccer objective:***
  1. covering by E.

❑ **Exercise 3**
The players are arranged as in diagram 32.

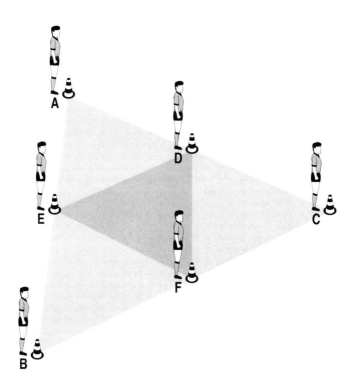

Diagram 32

This activity needs the movement of 4 players who change their positions as shown in diagram 33. When the coach gives a signal, A and B dribble the ball and get to the positions of D and F, who also move and dribble the ball to D_1 and F_1 on C's sides to rebuild the flipped form of the starting figure (C is the forward point of reference; E is the point of reference behind; A - B - D - F change their positions).

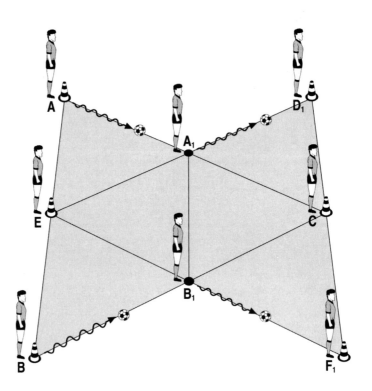

Diagram 33

- ■ *Soccer objective:*
    1. moving forward to get to positions along the same lines by following a restricted track.

❑ **Exercise 4**

In this exercise player E also moves: he gets to position E_1 in between A_1 and B_1.

Except for C, who acts as a point of reference, the other players are all involved in a forward movement (see diagram 34).

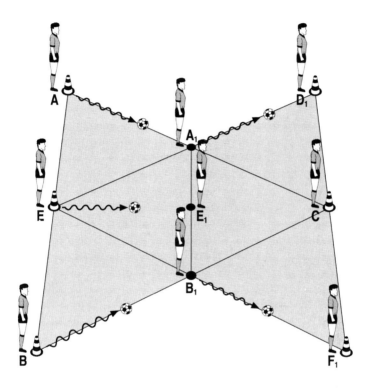

Diagram 34

- *Soccer objective:*
  1. moving forward to get to positions along the same lines by following a restricted track.

❏ **Exercise 5**

The players are arranged as shown in diagram 35: A - B - C at the corners of the big triangle, E - D - F at those of the inside one. First without and then with the ball, on the coach's signal, all the players move forward to solve the following problem: *"the 5 moving players must adapt their actions to any movement made by C, trying to maintain the characteristics of the starting figure"* - totality of the structure.

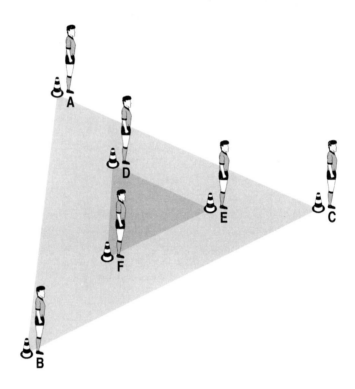

Diagram 35

By conforming to the movements of C, players A - B - D - E - F are all connected by a common objective.

It is vital to be able to play according to a common *"principle"* in a match. We can use the same method, this time using the ball, to apply a psychokinetic principle.

The previous 5 exercises show how at a youth level the geometric figure method is useful to carry out preparatory work for more difficult and targeted activities as the players mature.

The geometric figure is the *"informing guide"* to any motor action and acts as a support to develop that conscious awareness of space which F. Accame calls *"space proprioceptivity"*[2] and which is fundamental to solving the problems determined by the relationhip of *"team"* to *"space"*.

If applied to the geometric figures, the contents of Table D can give the opportunity to practice numerous activities (*"principle of variation"*).

---

[2] The elements of the geometric figures must be considered as *"indexes of awareness"* used to build....

❏ **Exercise 6**

The players are arranged as shown in diagram 36: A - B - C each have
a ball and are respectively placed opposite D - F - E.

When the coach gives the signal, A - B - C pass the ball to the
teammates opposite and sprint to change their positions at the corners
of the big triangle (counterclockwise in this case, see diagram 36).

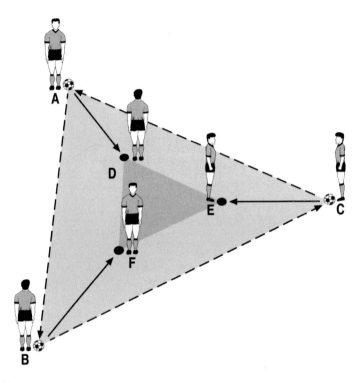

Diagram 36

Now players D - E - F have the ball (diagram 37). They pass it respectively to C_1 - B_1 - A_1 and sprint to change their positions at the corners of the inside triangle (counterclockwise in this case). Then the exercise continues.

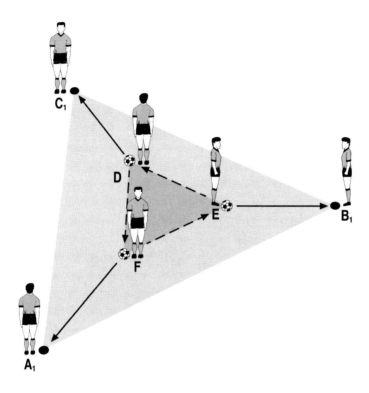

Diagram 37

The following is a variation of this exercise: the players are arranged as in diagram 36, with A - B - C having the ball. They carry out a one-two pass with their teammate opposite, then dribble the ball to the next corner (either clockwise or counterclockwise, according to what has been pre-established), as shown in diagram 38.

Psychokinetic principle applied: player A carries out a one-two pass choosing time and space (direction); the other two pairs react to the choice made.

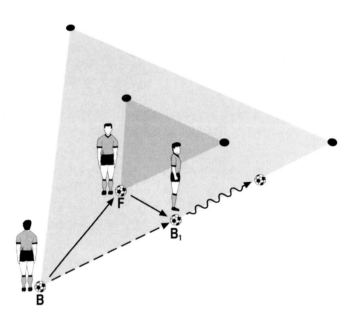

Diagram 38 - Only the movements of B and F are shown.

Competitions, like the next exercise, can also be introduced.

❑ **Exercise 7**

Six players with a ball are arranged as shown in diagram 39. "*How many passes can D - E - F make while A - B - C dribble the ball twice around the triangle?*"

The tasks are then reversed.

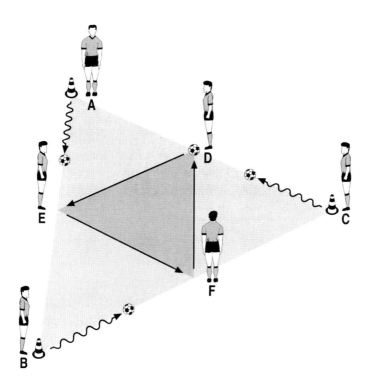

Diagram 39

At first the players of the inside triangle play with only one ball. Then, according to their skills, they can use two or even three balls.

Numerous technical elements can be applied in this exercise.

❑   **Exercise 8**
Let's start from Exercise 7, but without the ball, and count the laps run by A - B - C and E - F - D respectively in a given time.
After complete recovery roles are reversed.
In this way the exercise is useful for condition training. If during the exercise we introduce the change of direction (by a whistle, from clockwise to counterclockwise or viceversa) then we can practice another fundamental aspect: *"reactivity"*.

Almost all the exercises aimed at developing conditioning skills are specifically planned in the 11 to 12-year-old group.

Experience shows that it is better to play on a 16-yard equilateral triangle, considering that a 12-year-old player takes on average 25/30 seconds to dribble the ball twice all along the figure.

* *a 16-yard equilateral triangle;*
* *20/30 sec. "quick" work with the ball;*
* *alternate work/recovery;*
* *alternate phases of "play", to develop conditioning skills, with phases of work, to improve and consolidate technical-tactical aspects.*

The above 3 exercises have also been shown to develop *"conditioning skills"*. This is a further demonstration that geometric figures enable the coaching of every aspect of soccer.

Chapter 6

EXPERIENCES

❑ The experience at "Valconca 95" Soccer School
❑ The experience at San Marino Soccer League

The experience at "Valconca 95" Soccer School

Introduction

In their early age, young players tend to group around the ball during the matches. Tactical education means passing from this first attitude to the player's ability to play in the field, finding his position in the space according to his role, to the ball, to his teammates and opponents. This, together with technical, coordination and conditioning processes, must be one of the main objectives in the coaching of young players.

> *"Development, consolidation and education to the tactical aspect must be obtained through instruments and methods considering the young player's mental maturation, offering him forms of knowledge respectful of his degree of consciousness", op. cit.*

When planning activities and exercises the coach should consider the following **fundamental steps**:

1) *THE PLAYER AND THE SPACE OF PLAY*

- **Objective:**
  Knowing and recognizing the space of play

  - the shape of the field;
  - the length of the field (the goal lines);
  - the width of the field (the sidelines);
  - the midfield (the midfield line);
  - the inside spaces: the penalty area, the goal area, the midfield circle, the four corners;
  - the goals.

2) *THE PLAYER INSIDE THE FIELD*

- **Objective:**
  Representing and directing one's own body in the space of play

    - position of the child with regard to the space of play (sidelines, goal lines, midfield line etc.);
    - relations of proximity, distance and inclusion with regard to the limits of the space of play.

3) *THE PLAYER INSIDE THE FIELD WITH HIS TEAMMATES*

- **Objective:**
  Representing and directing one's own body in the space of play with regard to one's teammates

    - relations of inclusion, proximity and distance and with regard to the space of play and the teammates;
    - distance, lining-up and geometric figures;
    - introduction of roles, with exercises to help the child understand the tasks of defenders, midfielders and attackers (besides goalkeepers), know and recognize the three sections: defense, midfield, attack.

4) *ROLES AND PATTERNS OF PLAY*

> **In this context, "patterns" does not have exactly the same meaning it usually has: here it means "shape", "arrangement", "structure".**

- **Objective:**
  Knowing certain patterns of play and using new terms to define roles

    - the goalkeeper;
    - the defenders: right, center-right, left, center-left;
    - the midfielders: center-right, center, center-left;
    - the attackers: right, center, left.

5) THE PLAYER INSIDE THE FIELD WITH HIS TEAMMATES, AGAINST AN OPPOSING PLAYER WITH THE BALL

- **Objective:**
  Positioning oneself in the field

  - maintaining the role, connections with players of the same section and between sections;
  - mirror-like movements;
  - mirror-like movements with regard to the opponent with the ball and defense of one's own half of the field and goal.

6) THE PLAYER INSIDE THE FIELD WITH HIS TEAMMATES, AGAINST AN OPPOSING TEAM WITH THE BALL

- **Objective:**
  Positioning oneself in the field according to real play

THIS METHOD RELIES ON PARTICIPATORY MANAGEMENT OF THE GROUP THROUGH CORRECT AND CONTINUOUS COACH-PLAYER COMMUNICATION.

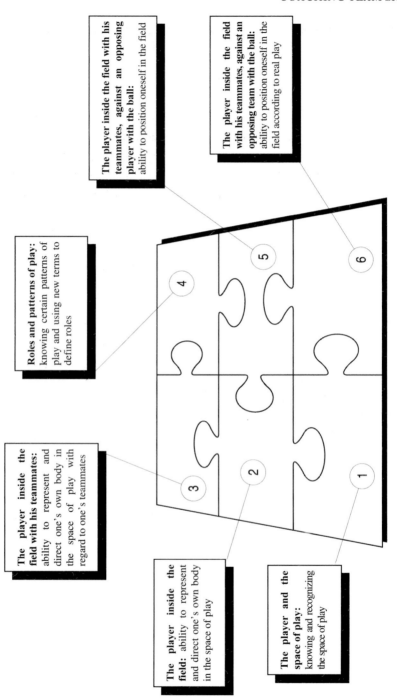

The player inside the field with his teammates, against an opposing player with the ball: ability to position oneself in the field

The player inside the field with his teammates, against an opposing team with the ball: ability to position oneself in the field according to real play

Roles and patterns of play: knowing certain patterns of play and using new terms to define roles

The player inside the field with his teammates: ability to represent and direct one's own body in the space of play with regard to one's teammates

The player inside the field: ability to represent and direct one's own body in the space of play

The player and the space of play: knowing and recognizing the space of play

Diagram 40 – Steps (6) and their related objectives conclude the logical and gradual sequence of coaching phases.

Table E is a summary of the fundamental steps and their objectives:

FUNDAMENTAL STEPS	OBJECTIVES
1) The player and the space of play	• Knowing and recognizing the space of play
2) The player inside the field	• Representing and directing one's own body in the space of play
3) The player inside the field with his teammates	• Representing and directing one's own body in the space of play with regard to one's teammates
4) Roles and patterns of play	• Knowing certain patterns of play and using new terms to define roles
5) The player inside the field with his teammates, against an opposing player with the ball	• Positioning oneself in the field
6) The player inside the field with his teammates, against an opposing team with the ball	• Positioning oneself in the field according to real play

Table E

FIRST STEP: The Player and the Space of Play

■ *Objective: Knowing and recognizing the space of play*

The objective of the first exercises is to make young players aware of the basic elements of the soccer field: goal lines, sidelines, midfield lines, penalty area lines, goal area lines, the midfield circle, goals, corners, etc.
Exercises:

• running along the lines that mark the soccer field;
• dribbling the ball along the lines that mark the soccer field, etc.

During the exercises, the players should be stimulated by asking them questions such as:

• Where are we running?
• What is the line opposite the one we are running on?
• What is this line called?
• What is the shape of the soccer field?
• What is the shape of the two areas of play? Etc.

Considering that the "under 10" age groups play matches in a smaller field and in a smaller number (5 against 5 in the 7-8 age group, 7 against 7 in the 9-10 age group), the young player must also get used to these smaller spaces.

For this purpose, a smaller field is usually marked in width and length inside the regular size soccer field, with smaller goals. This new space can be used for other exercises to stimulate and help the young players to know and recognize the space where they play:

a. dribbling the ball along the sidelines and goal lines;
b. dribbling the ball from one goal line to the one opposite;
c. dribbling the ball from one sideline to the one opposite;
d. dribbling the ball from the sideline to the goal line on their left/right;
e. dribbling the ball from the goal line to the midfield line;
f. dribbling the ball from the goal line to the center of the field;
g. dribbling the ball in single file from one corner (shown by the coach) to the one opposite.

Sometimes some children might not be able to do what they are requested, especially when the exercises are carried out on unmarked areas: we should intervene and ask stimulating questions whenever we realize that a player is hesitating or has doubts and follows a teammate without trying to understand.

The players usually have two attitudes to what the coach requests of them:

1) Active attitude: they try to put into practice what they have learned from the explanation and ask questions when the exercise is not clear. This is what we can call a positive attitude: the player moves in a critical and reflexive way, trying to find answers to his questions.

2) Passive attitude: it is typical of insecure children, who look at teammates and imitate them. The coach must intervene and help them understand the movements of the exercise.

The following can be suitable stimulating questions in a new situation:

- What is the shape of the new area of play?
- What are the missing limits? Etc.

Once the player has learned and recognizes the various limits of a smaller soccer field, we can turn his attention to its inside spaces:

- dribbling the ball inside the midfield circle;
- dribbling the ball inside the midfield circle trying to occupy all the space: when the coach whistles, the players stop the ball with the sole of the foot and check the occupation of space, etc.;
- starting from the line of the midfield circle, dribbling the ball to the center and back to the starting position;
- dribbling the ball inside the penalty area;
- dribbling the ball inside the goal area;
- dribbling the ball in the space between the line of the midfield circle and the penalty area;
- dribbling the ball near the right or left side line; etc.

Thanks to these simple exercises the player can learn and recognize the area of play; he will be able to recognize the limits and the inside spaces of the field, acquiring a specific language to define its elements.

SECOND STEP: The Player Inside the Field

- *Objective: Representing and directing one's own body in the space of play*

The previous exercises are aimed at providing the players with a good vision of the area of play, enabling them to learn and recognize the characteristics and the inside and outside limits of a soccer field.

The objective of the following exercises is to teach the ability to find one's bearings in the field and representation.

Here are some examples to better understand how to accomplish this second objective.

Example I   Imagine we are hikers and have lost our compass: how can we find our bearings without it?

A good hiker can understand where he is even without instruments; he only needs a watch, then nature provides the rest: the sun and the stars are good substitutes for the compass, at least in the less elaborated measurements. He can also find his bearings without the sun or the stars, by considering other elements: the presence of moss on trees and rocks, the most abundant snow and snow at low altitude, the most developed undergrowth, the higher limits of the mountains that indicate north, cleaner stones, dry rocks, less snow, the lower limits of vegetation that indicate south.

Example I I Let's ask the player this question: where are we now?

I mean where the soccer field is located, that is in ....(town), near the river ...., between the ... district and .... street, etc.

The objective of the question is to make the player understand that our position in the space is not absolute, but is defined by points of reference.

If you should explain to somebody where you live, what would you tell him or her?

Of course the answer varies according to the individual; the coach should keep on stimulating the players to guide them to the objective, which is to answer the following question: where are we now with regard to the area of play?

(The players should be in the field, preferably far from the
lines of reference).

On the basis of their previous reasoning, the players will try
to find those points of reference that enable them to find their
bearings and representation in the space considered: for
example, I am near..., or between the ... line and the ... line,
or inside ..., close to ..., etc.

Relations of inclusion, nearness and distance will start to build up
according to the players' degree of mental maturation. The objective will
be accomplished once the player takes up the position required by the
coach and can verbally express it.

Question: "*Where are you?*"

Answer: "*I am near the right sideline, between the midfield line and the
penalty area line*" (see diagram 41).

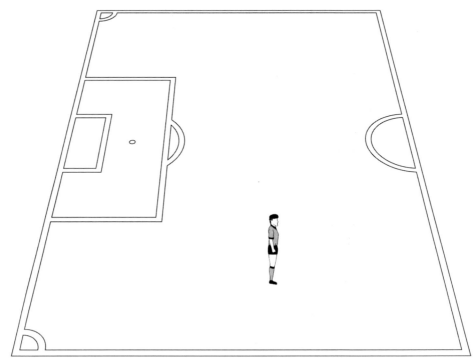

Diagram 41

The coach can use some exercises with verbal instructions to practice positioning in the field, for example:

- dribble the ball from where you are up to inside the penalty area in front of you, closer to the right corner;
- dribble the ball to the place you prefer, then explain where you are.

The player now can explain his position and has understood relations of inclusion, nearness and distance.

It is important to remember that in these first two steps the objective is knowing, recognizing and finding one's bearings in the area of play, first in a regular size field then in a smaller one. Therefore, the coaching progression should be as follows:

1. exercises in a regular size field;
2. exercises in a smaller field;
3. exercises based on a comparison of the two fields.

THIRD STEP: The Player Inside the Field with His Teammates

▪ *Objective: Representing and directing one's own body in the space of play with regard to one's teammates*

The objective of this third step is to stimulate a rational occupation of the area of play without repressing the players' continuous search for the possession of the ball.

Exercises:
- the players are divided into groups of three: when the coach gives the signal they form the first geometric figure, the triangle, within a pre-established time;
- the exercise is repeated, forming bigger or smaller triangles; mistakes must be corrected;
- the players are divided into groups of four: they must form the second geometric figure, the square;
- then, the players must form the third geometric figure, the rhombus (when coaching 6-8 year olds they might not know this figure: in that case they can be required to form a kite);
- the players are divided into groups of more than four: they must form the same figures as before;
- the players must form a circle.

Usually they do not find it difficult to form a triangle, a square or a rhombus if the number of players is equal to the number of sides (or corners) of the figure.
They can run into difficulties when:
- the number of players is superior to the number of sides of the figure;
- they are required to form more complex figures.

Once the players know, recognize and form the above geometric figures, they can use them in the area of play with exercises where the connections and characteristics are maintained.
After these exercises the players can play a small sided match to get familiar with positions/roles.

Divided into two five-player teams (4 plus the goalkeeper), the players are asked to play while using an arrangement corresponding to one of the previous geometric figures. As there are 4 of them, they are usually asked to choose either the square or the rhombus.

The coach can ask stimulating questions, such as:

- Is it better to play arranged in a square or in a rhombus?
- What is the difference between these two figures?
- What roles can we notice in the square-shaped arrangement?
- What roles can we notice in the rhombus-shaped arrangement?

The discussion, guided by the coach, will lead the players to choose the rhombus as in this figure soccer roles can easily be identified.

During the match, the coach must verbally remind the players to maintain the figure, without interrupting the game. Each player must consider not only the ball but also his position with regard to his teammates so as to maintain the characteristics of the figure chosen and rationally occupy the area of play.

Let's take one step back now and ask a player:

"*Where are you now with regard to the area of play and your teammates?*" "*What is your position?*"

His numerous points of reference now enable him to better find his bearings. His answer:

"*I am near the right sideline, I am a right midfielder, in front of me I have the attacker and the defender is behind*" (see diagram 42).

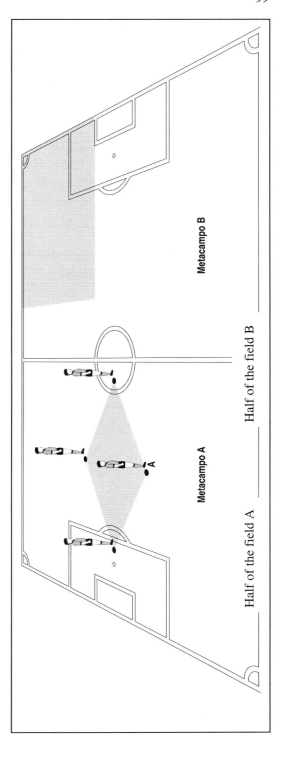

Diagram 42 - Half of the field A shows the position of player A; Half of the field B shows the 5 against 5 area of play (according to the measures of a regular-size field).

In this way the player can understand and become aware of the meaning of his role. If he plays as a midfielder he knows that he must position at a certain distance between the forwards and the defenders in order to maintain the arrangement.

FOURTH STEP: Roles and Patterns of Play

▪ *Objective: Knowing certain patterns of play and using new terms to define roles*

"What is my role?"
This is the most recurring question before any match; the answer involves an exact indication of what the player's tasks will be during the game.
The player might not know the meaning of such words as *halfback*, *sweeper* or *left back*: it is better if we use the following terms:

- goalkeeper;
- defenders: center, center-right, center-left, extreme right, extreme left;
- midfielders: center, center-right, center-left;
- attackers: center, right, left.

These definitions are easier as they directly refer to the arrangement and organization of the team.

❑ **Examples**

1) 7-8 age group - 5 against 5 - team in a "rhombus-shaped" (or "kite-shaped") arrangement (see diagram 43)

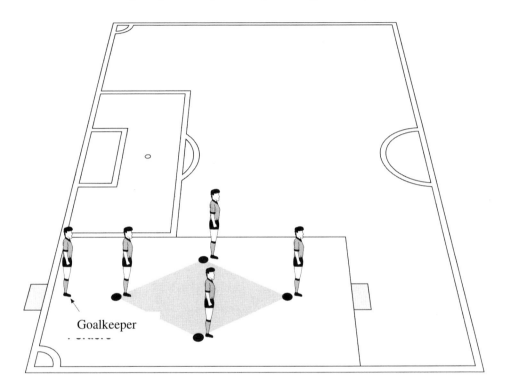

Goalkeeper

Diagram 43

Roles:
1. tail of the kite = central defender;
2. right corner of the kite = right midfielder
3. left corner of the kite = left midfielder
4. top of the kite = central attacker.

2) 9-10 age group - 7 against 7 - team arranged according to a "pyramid with inner triangles" (see diagram 44)

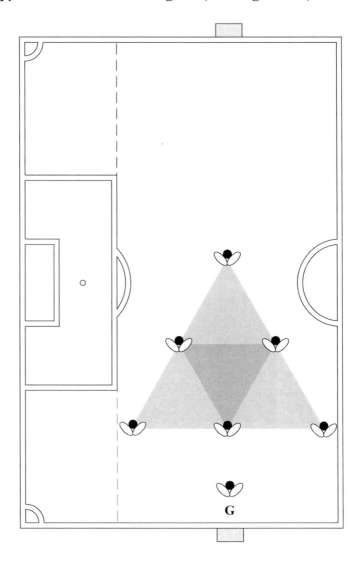

Diagram 44

Diagram 45 shows the "*rhombus + triangle*" arrangement (Sector B), which is coached together with the "*pyramid + inner triangles*"[3] (Sector A).

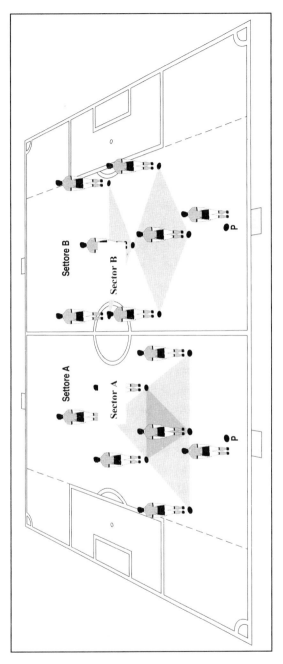

Diagram 45

---

[3] The players usually learn this figure quite easily but have problems in maintaining their connections during the play. Experience shows that this is a very important figure to coach, develop and improve.

Roles:
a. base of the pyramid = defenders:
    1. right corner = extreme right defender;
    2. left corner = extreme left defender;
    3. middle of the base of the pyramid = central defender.

b. Central part of the pyramid = midfielders
    4. top corner of the triangle formed with the extreme right defender and the central defender = center-right midfielder;
    5. top corner of the triangle formed with the extreme left defender and the central defender = center-left midfielder.

c. Top of the pyramid = attackers:
    6. central attacker.

The *7 against 7* pyramid-shaped arrangement is a remarkable step forward from the *5 against 5* "kite": the player can recognize situations of play that he will later find in the "*11 against 11*". During the game the players must maintain:

*   the relations of nearness-distance-inclusion between the defense, midfield and attack sections;
*   the relations of nearness-distance-inclusion between the players of the same section;
*   the pyramid-shaped arrangement;
*   the pyramid inner triangle arrangement.

The definition of center-right and center-left midfielder considers the necessity of letting the wings free for the two defenders who are therefore called "extreme right" and "extreme left" defenders.

This provides a higher number of attacking players, which is more fun and is a tactical organization that will be very helpful in the "*11 against 11*".

The arrangement of the three defenders along the same line gets them used to the concept of "lining-up" and also for the future introduction of a fourth defender.

The role of "forward" is usually given to the player who, besides having certain technical and offensive skills, is less sure than his teammates about space positioning and therefore is given more freedom.

The two "midfielders" usually run into difficulties as they tend to get onto the wings too far from each other. These difficulties are normal, as their role requires the ability to maintain a higher number of connections; besides, in the smaller field there are no such reference points as the "midfield circle" or "line" to help them.

For a correct and logical space progression, I think the size of the field should be increased according to the technical, physical and positioning abilities of the players. In fact, it is true that the smaller field enables the player to play the ball more often, but at the same time it cuts down the time available to make decisions about the situations of play. An 8-10-year-old child can find it difficult to control a ball passed to him at a certain speed and from a short distance, and he can hardly act consciously without enough time and space.

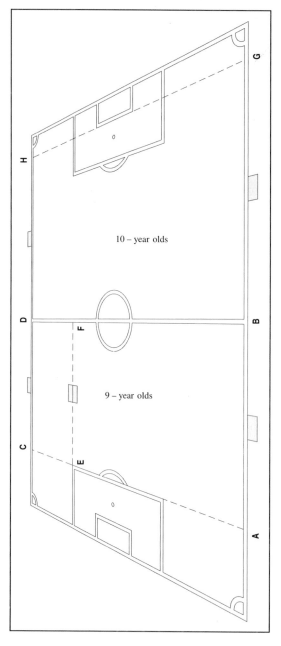

10 – year olds

9 – year olds

As a consequence, with 9-10 year olds ("*7 against 7*") I divided the field as shown in diagram 46.

I started with the A - B - F - E rectangle, adding later the E - F - C - D space (the A - B - C - D rectangle is the space recommended by the FIGC - Italian Soccer League).

Then, when the older players in this age group played at home I used the B - G - H - D rectangle (at first the coaches and players of the opposing teams were surprised, but then they favorably accepted the "*new*" space after my explanation).

Diagram 46

3) 11 to 12-year-old age group - 11 against 11 - "4-4-2" arrangement
(see diagram 47)

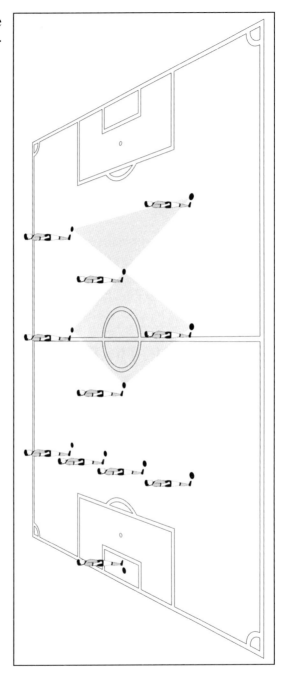

Diagram 47

Roles:
1. defensive lining-up = extreme right defender, center-right defender, center-left defender, extreme left defender;
2. midfield rhombus:
   a. bottom corner = defensive central midfielder;
   b. right corner = center-right midfielder;
   c. left corner = center-left midfielder;
   d. top corner = offensive central midfielder;
3. base of the triangle formed by the two attackers with the offensive central midfielder: right corner = right attacker; left corner = left attacker.

In this way the player can immediately find his position thanks to the points of reference he already knows. This also enables the coach to shift the players to different roles without too much difficulty, favoring the development of a flexible, *"universal"*[4] player.

FIFTH STEP: The Player Inside the Field with His Teammates, Against an Opposing Player with the Ball

- *Objective: Positioning oneself in the field*

In this phase the exercises are carried out with the following elements:
- an opponent with the ball;
- the goal as a point of reference of primary importance, both in case of possession and non-possession of the ball.

The players can carry out all those exercises that require mirror-like movements with regard to an opponent with the ball, aiming at stealing the ball and defending the goal.

---

[4] In this context, *"universal"* means that at the end of the development period, the child knows and puts into practice correct tactical movements in any part of the field.

SIXTH STEP: The Player Inside the Field with His Teammates, Against an Opposing Team with the Ball

- *Objective: Positioning oneself in the field according to real play*

In this phase the "*real*" match on a regular size field starts. The "*space*" of the geometric figures makes room for concepts and connections "*learned*" during practice.

The players' movements and connections show individual, "*conscious*" actions inserted in a framework of team action.

Appendix

Passing from 7 against 7 (9-10-year-old age group) to 11 against 11 (11-12 age group) = passing from a pyramid-shaped arrangement to 11 players arranged according to the 4-4-2 (exercise for 10-12 year olds)
Outlines for progressive coaching enabling the players to position themselves in the field and adapt to the new space situation (regular size field) and higher number of players (11).

Passing from a 7-player to an 11-player arrangement should not be too difficult for a child, provided he has been coached using the "*pyramid-shaped*" game in the 9-10 age group.

In fact, he needs to develop and continue that coaching process started in the 7 against 7.

Difficulties are mostly due to:
1) the higher number of players;
2) the larger size of the field.

1) There are four new players: one extra player in the defense, for a defensive line made up of four players, two of whom are central defenders (center-right and center-left); two extra midfielders, for a rhombus-quadrilateral made up of four midfielders; one extra attacker, for an attack made up of two players.

2) The area of play is larger and with new limits, not marked in the 7 against 7:
   • the penalty and goal areas;
   • the midfield circle.

The new exercises must consider these new elements and their characteristics: a *"coaching progression"* must be started, either based on the principle of knowing, recognizing and finding position in the new area of play, or on the principle of the introduction of the new players, the formation of new sections and their relationships to each other.

❑ **Coaching progression: 11 players in movement**

1) Visualize the new pattern of play on a board and/or use photos or videos; explain the new relationships between sections and players of the same section; get the players acquainted with the terms used to define the new roles they are going to be given.
2) After putting markers on the field to show the players' positions, arrange the eleven players maintaining the 7 against 7 area of play; then, carry out mirror-like exercises in which great care must be taken to maintain the new distances between the sections and between players of the same section.
3) Practice mirror-like[5] exercises for the sections.
4) Practice mirror-like exercises with all 11 players in the field.
5) Carry out mirror-like exercises involving the following sections:
   • defense and midfield;
   • midfield and attack.
   During these exercises great care must be taken to maintain the distances and the relationships between the sections (concept of balance). Stimulate effective verbal communication between players to form and maintain the *"structure"*. One or two children per section could be chosen to act as verbal guides and points of reference for their teammates: they are usually the central defender for the defense and the defending central midfielder for the midfield.

_____

[5] With *"mirror-like movements"* I mean moving while maintaining relationships with the teammates of the section, not movements aimed at the defensive and offensive phase of the play.

6) Repeat the exercises in point 2 above to see if improvements have been made and then *"transfer"* them to the regular size field.

❑ **Coaching progression: the real field**

1) **Knowing and recognizing the area of play:**
   - exercises while running with or without the ball, to make the player explore the new space;
   - exercises as above, along the lines limiting the spaces of the play area: midfield circle, penalty areas, goal areas, etc.;
   - while running with the ball, when the coach gives the signal the players try to occupy all the spaces of the field within a pre-established time;
   - while running with the ball, when the coach gives the signal the players occupy the whole penalty area;
   - while running with the ball, when the coach gives the signal the players occupy one half of the field, etc.

2) **Geometric figures:**
   - exercises with the triangle, square, rhombus and their related structures;
   - mirror-like movements;
   - practicing geometric figures inside the area of play;
   - exercises about transformation of the geometric figures in a lining-up, diagonal arrangement, etc.

3) **Introduction of the exercises of the *"11 players in movement"* coaching progression**

Communication

Adequate, functional and understandable communication between the coach and the players is fundamental, in a *"participatory management"* which is useful to both coach and players.

During both coaching sessions and championship matches, it is quite frequent to hear a coach *"guide"* his players with the following expressions:

"Shift";
"Cover";
"Return to your position";
"Carry out the diagonal";
"Go";
"Return";
"You must stay here";
"Why are you going there?"
"You must be a forward"; etc.

These sentences show lack of *"participatory management"*: the language used consists of orders for the player to carry out. It is better to use suggestions with different words, for example:
"Look at where you are";
"Remember the figure";
"What is your position?";
"Where are your section teammates?";
"Where is the ball?";
"Run towards the ball"; etc.

In this way we give advice and points of reference to stimulate the player to give adequate motor responses through mental operations: he reflects, finds the possible mistake and corrects it.

> **The match acquires coaching meaning and represents the highest form of exercise aimed at coaching the "ability of positioning oneself in the field".**

Through communication the match acquires *"coaching meaning"* and represents the highest form of exercise aimed at coaching the "ability of positioning oneself in the field".

Conclusion

The objective of this coaching method is to teach the player to position himself in the field, that is, to help him find his position in the area of play with regard to ball, role, teammates and opponents, and make him aware of his actions.

Why pursue this objective starting with 8-9 year olds? Is it not too early to talk about tactical organization? Coaching any content is never untimely if it is respectful of the child's mental maturation phases.

> *Coaching any content is never untimely if it is respectful of the child's mental maturation phases.*

Primary school math teachers start teaching geometry when the children are six years old, introducing the first space elements (sets, "inside and outside", "in front and behind", "over and under", etc.); the simpler geometric figures are introduced when the children are 7: they are required to recognize, draw and find figures that can be found in objects within their environment.

The knowledge of geometric figures improves when the children are 8. At this age they can draw the figures with more precision and can solve simple problems about side measurements, perimeters, kinds of angles, etc.

This method helps the child to play. How?

In the phase when the child overcomes egocentricity to establish relations with others and "*work*" with them, he needs to set simple rules to make the game develop with more order: he wants to participate and identify himself with a task for which he is responsible.

In our case, this means not only should we simplify the rules of the game, reduce the size of the field and the number of the players, but we should also give the child a task, his **role**. The role becomes a necessity for him. He wants to identify himself with actions which are his and for which he is responsible.

> *The role becomes a necessity for the child. He wants to identify himself with actions which are his and for which he is responsible.*

Giving a role to the child requires the teaching of related operations in order to make him become aware of his task. In addition, during the play, the roles guarantee the child's actions by providing a framework for "*orderly play*".

Watching some 9-10 age group matches, I noticed the following:

1) The *"less clever"* and less assertive players do not touch the ball very often and show hesitation when they move in the field.
2) The *"more clever"* and assertive ones touch the ball very often and are the protagonists of the match.
3) The children who play without roles form groups and do not occupy the field rationally, thus missing the opportunity to carry out correct movements.
4) The children who are given a role according to *"traditional principles"* hesitate while moving, while carrying out the task they have been given. Some children do not move, remaining still to occupy what for them is their role, that is the place where the coach put them at the beginning (these are the less assertive and more insecure children); others, after maintaining their position for some minutes without touching the ball, forget their role and go towards the ball or the point of reference that attracts them the most.

In these situations, communication by the coach is usually made up of the following expressions to *"correct"* them:

"Where are you going?";

"You must stay in the midfield";

"You are a defender";

"You must pass the ball, you cannot do everything on your own";

"You must stay there";

"Run";

"Pass it to ... ";

"Kick it away"; etc.

These are orders for actions that the child does not understand but performs passively: they show the lack of participatory management of the group and the use of a language which is not common to both subjects - coach and players.

The method we propose remedies the above errors and helps the child when he plays because:

- he knows the area of play and the terms related to it;
- he can understand where he is, having as a point of reference the lines of the field and his teammates, not only the ball;
- he has some exact points of reference to which to pay attention, common to all the members of the team;
- when he chooses his *"role"*, he knows the rules that enable him to respect it: this gives him freedom to act and move within an

arrangement agreed upon by everybody and with which all the players identify themselves;

- the children's different personalities are balanced to everybody's advantage: the most assertive and enterprising children will hold back in order to respect the tasks connected with their role, while the less secure and less assertive will be "*pushed*" to act in order to respect the tasks connected with their role, without the coach's verbal order.

The examples and the exercises related to the steps we have considered mostly concern the player "*not in possession of the ball*": this is to focus the player's attention on the points of reference and accomplish the pre-established objectives.

The choice of the arrangement of the team according to the suggested roles and patterns assists the player also when he is "*in possession of the ball*": during a match, his awareness of his role and position on the field helps him simplify the amount of visual information he must process and to make the right decision in the numerous situations of play.

The player is aware of his teammates' position and so adapts his behavior to actual situations, relying on known and stable points of reference.

The experience related was made at "Scuola Calcio Valconca 95" by teacher of Physical Education and coach Fabio Lepri from 1993 to 1998. This soccer school was attended by players living in Mercatino Conca, Montecerignone, Montegrimano and Sassofeltrio, in the Pesaro district.

Other contributions witnessing the methos applied have been made by:
Loris Bonesso;
Paolo Borioni;
Samuele Carloni;
Domenico Cascione;
Cosimo D'Angelo;
Francesco Magnani;
Raffaele Matulli;
Francesco Moroni;
Antonio Palmisano;
Maurizio Pisani;
Fiorenzo Pettinari;
Maurizio Pozzi;
Roberto Rabboni;
Pinto Vito.

The experience at
the San Marino Soccer League

In September 1994 Giorgio Crescentini, chairman of the San Marino Soccer League, called me to the League's premises to talk about the idea of a project for the youth sector.

He described the situation, the available structures and the policy the League Council had decided to adopt. Objectives, programs and tasks were to be considered, assessed and defined.

I accepted the offer to study the project for two reasons: first, because it pursued middle and long term objectives; second, because it was mostly centered on players between 6 and 12 years old.

So, supported by the whole League Council (Giorgio Crescentini, Pierluigi Ceccoli, Luciano Casadei, Marco Guidi, Giorgio Giardi, Josef Guidi, Maurizio Montironi) and in close cooperation with the coaches and managers of all the clubs, I set out a middle and long term plan defining objectives, activities, contents, methods and instruments.

My task as Technical Coordinator for the youth sector was twofold: first, be in the field with the players and their respective coaches to practice the contents and the planned coaching sequences; second, watch and analyze the activity, together with the coaches and managers, in order to update and suggest different solutions when certain activities did not yield appreciable results.

Over the years, especially with the manager of the youth sector Maurizio Montironi, I refined methods and investigated themes and objectives. This proceeding was not simple: sometimes it raised doubts, hesitation and moments of indifference. There were obstacles and misunderstandings. These were overcome, however, by the fact that every change was made first considering the development of the child, and then of the young soccer player. All this was fitted into the main objective:

"the promotion of the image of the League as a sports promotion system useful for improving sports culture, working for the education and development of the citizen".

For the 1998/1999 soccer season this process can be summed up in the following tables.

Table F shows the *"Development objectives"* defined in the 1996/1997 soccer season.

Table G shows the *"Organization chart"* (defined in the 1998/1999 soccer season) promoted and managed by the League, which is totally responsible for it.

Table H explains the *"plan for coaching the geometric figures"*. Its phases have been defined thanks to the opportunities I had to try out their use and application. After putting into practice contents and methods, and following up the development (even if not always directly and with all the coaches), I analyzed and constantly checked whether the objectives were accomplished or not.

I am proud to say that the insights I had many years ago about breaking new ground for the tactical development of the young player were and are valid, useful and applicable to soccer.

This is why I will never be able to sufficiently express my "thanks" to the players, coaches, collaborators and League council of San Marino.

OBJECTIVES OF DEVELOPMENT (1996/1997 soccer season)

AGE	COACHING	FUNDAMENTAL SKILLS	TECHNICAL	TACTICAL	PHYSICAL	PSYCHO-PEDAGOGIC	COMMUNICATION
6/7/8 YEARS OLD (PRE FORMATION)	2 sessions a week 3 / 4 hours a week		Command of the ball: - touch; - control; - dribble; - protection; - possession.	Games aiming at building the outside and specific space of soccer: - the attack; - the defense; - the teammates; - the opponents; - cooperation.	Motor coordination; Joint mobility; Reaction speed; Awareness of one's own body in both static and dynamic situations	Being together; Fun and play; Moral value of the rule	
9/10 YEARS OLD (INTRODUCTION)	2 sessions a week 3 / 4 hours a week		All the fundamental skills in conditions of applied skills	**Functional space prerequisites with regard to soccer**	Neuro-muscular and coordination development	From games... to soccer; The group	
11/12 YEARS OLD (PRODUCTION)	2 / 3 sessions a week 4 / 5 hours a week		Applied skills in real play (with teammates and opponents)	Fundamental skills: - possession of the ball; - non-possession of the ball; - change of possession; - situations of play; - organization of play.	Conditioning abilities activation and development	The team; Competition; Victory and defeat	

IMPROVING THE SKILLS FOR BETTER TACTICS

Table F

ORGANIZATION CHART OF THE YOUTH SECTOR (1998/1999 SOCCER SEASON)

AGE	AGE GROUP	KIND OF COMPETITION	AREA OF PLAY	NUMBER OF PLAYERS	TIME	RULES
6/8 YEARS OLD	MINICALCIO	TOURNAMENTS	GYM - 5 A SIDE SOCCER FIELD	5 AGAINST 5	SITUATIONS AND CHANGES LIKE IN BASKETBALL	SAN MARINO SOCCER LEAGUE
8/9 YEARS OLD	PRIMICALCI	TOURNAMENTS	GYM - 5 A SIDE SOCCER FIELD	5 AGAINST 5	SITUATIONS AND CHANGES LIKE IN BASKETBALL	SAN MARINO SOCCER LEAGUE
9/10 YEARS OLD	UNDER 10	AUTUMN AND SPRING CHAMPIONSHIP	ABOUT 65X45 YARDS	7 AGAINST 7	2 15-MINUTE HALVES	SAN MARINO SOCCER LEAGUE
11/12 YEARS OLD	UNDER 12	AUTUMN AND SPRING CHAMPIONSHIP	ABOUT 75X55	9 AGAINST 9	2 30-MINUTE HALVES	SAN MARINO SOCCER LEAGUE
13/15 YEARS OLD	UNDER 15	AUTUMN AND SPRING CHAMPIONSHIP	REGULAR SIZE FIELD	11 AGAINST 11	2 35-MINUTE HALVES	SAN MARINO SOCCER LEAGUE
NATIONAL SELECTION	UNDER 16	EUROPEAN CHAMPIONSHIP	REGULAR SIZE FIELD	11 AGAINST 11	U.E.F.A. REGULAR TIME	U.E.F.A.
NATIONAL SELECTION	UNDER 18	EUROPEAN CHAMPIONSHIP	REGULAR SIZE FIELD	11 AGAINST 11	U.E.F.A. REGULAR TIME	U.E.F.A.
NATIONAL SELECTION	UNDER 18	"PAOLO VALENTI" TOURNAMENT	REGULAR SIZE FIELD	11 AGAINST 11	U.E.F.A.- F.I.G.C. REGULAR TIME	U.E.F.A.-F.I.G.C. (Italian Soccer League)
1985	GIOVANISSIMI PROVINCIALI	CHAMPIONSHIP	REGULAR SIZE FIELD	11 AGAINST 11	2 30-MINUTE HALVES	F.I.G.C.
1984	GIOVANISSIMI REGIONALI	CHAMPIONSHIP	REGULAR SIZE FIELD	11 AGAINST 11	2 30-MINUTE HALVES	F.I.G.C.
1983	ALLIEVI PROVINCIALI	CHAMPIONSHIP	REGULAR SIZE FIELD	11 AGAINST 11	2 40-MINUTE HALVES	F.I.G.C.
1982	ALLIEVI REGIONALI	CHAMPIONSHIP	REGULAR SIZE FIELD	11 AGAINST 11	2 40-MINUTE HALVES	F.I.G.C.

Table G

PLAN FOR COACHING THE GEOMETRIC FIGURES

MINICALCIO - PRIMICALCI - UNDER 10		UNDER 12 **	UNDER 15 *
7/8 years old - 5 against 5	9/10 years old - 7 against 7	11/12 years old - 9 against 9	13/14 years old - 11 against 11
1ˢᵗ year: - the area of play of the small sided match; - the goals; - the external lines and the ball: inside and outside. **2ⁿᵈ year:** - the kite; - staying in front of the goalkeeper; - staying on the right; - staying on the left; - staying in the center; - staying forward; - staying behind..	**1ˢᵗ year:** - the space of the small sided match; - all the lines; - nearness, inclusion and order relations; - from the kite to the rhombus; - the distance; - the lining-up; - the pyramid. **2ⁿᵈ year:** - the triangle; - triangles in a row; - triangles in a line; - the rhombus; - connections; - points of reference; - the pyramid and its inner triangles; - the rhombus and the diagonal; - the diagonal.	**1ˢᵗ/2ⁿᵈ year:** - the diagonal and the lining-up; - the pyramid and its inner triangles; - the rhombus and the triangle; - development and consolidation of the basic geometric figures.	**From the principles of the Geometric Figures to positioning oneself in the field... to tactical awareness... to tactical knowledge... to the intelligent player** COMPLETION AND CONSOLIDATION ACTIVITIES

LOGICAL GRADUALITY IN THE DEVELOPMENT

*: The age groups described refer to the ones established by the San Marino Soccer League and the Italian Soccer League respectively.

**: Some teams in this age group participate in the National Esordienti Championship in Italy, playing 11 against 11.

Table H

Conclusion
by Emilio Cecchini

After years of experience, "concepts" come to mind like frames, inspired by U.E.F.A. conventions[6], various readings, refresher courses, lessons at the Higher School of Physical Training at the University of Urbino, conversations with professional and non-professional youth soccer coaches, teachers, psychologists, activity with all those children with whom I have shared their and my own development. They are like a chorus with many voices expressing one selected objective: **coaches for soccer as a development factor, in favor of every child as if he were the center of the world.**

- Children must not be coached, they must be formed.
- During the forming process the child has distinct biological maturation times that must be considered and respected.
- Teaching/coaching should proceed from global to analytic and from analytic to global, and consider when, how and in what percentage each should be addressed.
- Play should be oriented to the acquisition of certain skills/abilities.
- Operational options should be provided to combine coordination and conditioning skills.
- Play should be considered as a means and not an end.
- The main objective should be to form creative, autonomous, inventive players.
- The coach should plan "*how*" to teach, not "*what*" to teach.
- The child should be taught to pass from a rigid movement structure to continuous adjustments, as there will never be the same conditions: the movement must be functional to the requirements.
- The coach is at the players' service: he makes learning easier, participates in the global forming process, wants to know, understand...and learn.
- The player should be placed in the situation, with rights, obligations and fundamental rules.

---

[6] I have the chance to participate in U.E.F.A. conventions as a collaborator of one of the smallest European leagues: the San Marino Soccer League.

- "I have the ball and I am the actor, I pass the ball and I become a spectator": this attitude must be changed in favor of an active and supporting one.
- A technical movement originates from play: method of play.
- Use play forms and matches to coach soccer. Simplified and modified play is the starting point for the coach, who will then look for the best way to coach play at higher levels in the quickest and most amusing way.
- Give a meaning to each coaching session and, at the end, ask yourself whether the objective has been accomplished.
- Try to emphasize more quality, less quantity.
- The coaching phases which are no fun are old-fashioned; in order to get better results coaching must be like a "soccer party".
- When teaching use any possible educational aid: sketches, graphs, simulations, videos, etc.
- Integrate and correlate work in the soccer field with theory.
- Soccer adapts to the player, not vice-versa.
- The learning process needs a lot of time.
- The coach should know himself and often apply self-criticism.
- Educating the child comes before forming the player.
- The coach must be able to understand the changes in society and in young people, so that he speaks their language and places himself on the same level, while at the same time remembering his own responsibilities and position.
- Everybody must have the opportunity to play: no discrimination.
- The top priority should be safety.
- The best coaches must take care of the youth sector.
- The coach should form and coach an offensive mentality, providing more opportunities to score.
- The coach should stimulate the will to score, rather than the will not to be scored against.
- The players should develop the ability to play with the opponent, not against.
- A coach "*feels*" he is such: it is like clothing one always wears.
- A good coach must have a knowledge of soccer and be an expert in human development.

- Make children play to develop the ability to play, then coach the basic elements as *"means"* to improve in time: first *"play"* and then *"fundamental skills"*, first *"tactics"* and then *"skills"*.
- Teach the children to *"act"* in a functional way to play.
- The coach should consider the *"result"* of the match in the right way...partly because every positive result motivates the player even more.
- Winning is not the most important thing: to get involved to win is the only thing that counts.
- Communicate, interact, exchange opinions with all the players. Pedagogy of questions.
- Move forward to attack, move forward to defend: when and how to teach this *"group organization"*?
- When I carry out a speed variation the opponent always runs into difficulties, and, when this kind of action is carried out by the whole team, it is as effective as possible. Quantity of play, pace, acceleration: at what age should these be coached?
- Continuous integration between technical, methodological and psychological aspects.
- Use a coaching method based on simple and modified forms of play, especially with the youngest players.
- Play is the coach's fundamental resource.
- Enliven the activities, convey the ideas through a personal style of work, stimulate each individual player's inventiveness.
- Always create a joyful atmosphere for optimum competitiveness.
- Soccer is an educational instrument and fun.
- Skills, play insight and communication can be distinguished but not separated. They are closely connected and interdependent.
- Educating, teaching and winning: it is possible.
- Create the conditions for better learning: soccer objectives, repetitions, much fun, numerous teaching opportunities.
- Every coaching progression must consider the teaching/learning factor.
- Form the players' character by developing their sportsmanship, self-discipline, self-confidence, courage and initiative.
- At first, for children, playing soccer means "to touch the ball". Then there is a golden rule: not *"skills"*, but command of the ball.
- Coach players to love the ball...the ball has a soul.
- Avoid early specialization and the search for positive results at any cost.

- 4 against 4 until the age of 8; 7 against 7 until 10; 9 against 9 until 12.
- Science does not kill inventiveness, it can but exalt its expression.
- Until the age of 12 respect a proportional relationship with area of play, goals and ball.
- It is always time to invest in young players.
- Coaching youth soccer: mixing coaching science and education art.
- Have an emotional behavior, "*coach*" the head, the heart, the soul...do not ignore emotions.
- The primary objective is a natural love for the game, for the positive values of life: stimulate young people, refine talents, strengthen will and happiness, joy of playing, pleasure of competition, enthusiasm, passion.
- Friendship is more important than results.
- In youth soccer, the "*figure*" of reference must be: a promoter, organizer, entertainer, teacher, coach, educator...all at the same time.
- Never interrupt the players' learning process.
- Soccer evolves continuously. One thing is constant in life: change.
- In the exercises, the tactical objective represents "*why*", the skills express "*how*".
- Define with the players a space and a time to be free and autonomous.
- Be on the same wave-length as the players.
- The space of logic in the various relationships covers the children's whole life: nothing can be educational, if not filtered by the brain.
- Assessment in order to know and educate is the main function of any educational process: assessment to select and then put aside is cruel and anti-pedagogic.

Final conclusion
By G. Trapattoni

At a U.E.F.A. convention in Barcelona (February 23-27, 1998), technical manager Andy Roxburgh discussed "the Philosophy of the Coach", using the material shown on the following pages (photos 1 and 2).
The objective was to see if, in the third millennium, a universal approach to *"soccer"* could be found by comparing the opinions of a U.E.F.A. technical manager, a high performance soccer coach and a youth soccer coach. Thus, starting from the human aspect (clockwise) the comparison has given the following results.

The coach must be compassionate in his relationships with his players, conveying understanding and positive feelings that influence the player as an individual and as a thinking, autonomous and inventive being. The coach must take risks, make mistakes, admit and correct them: this is part of human nature too.

A coach is inventive when he understands and sees the opportunities to develop all the abilities of his players: he can see their improvement, potential and effectiveness. The players can improve also when they are over 30, developing some characteristics that they probably did not know or practice before.

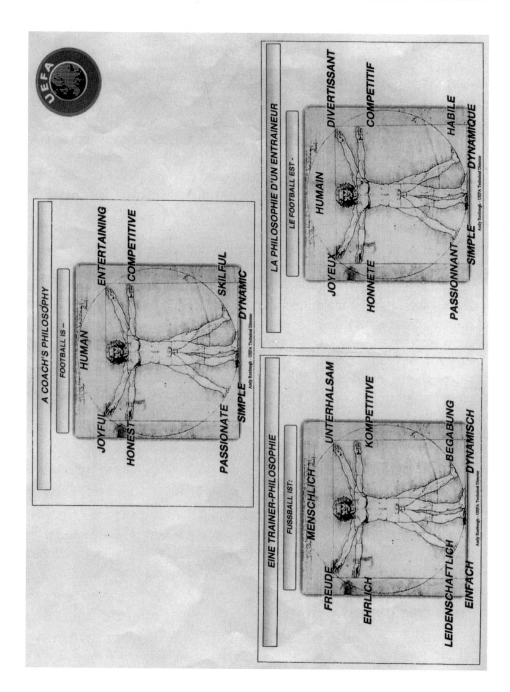

Photo 1

A COACH'S PHILOSOPHY

Football is -

1. **HUMAN**

   - art - not science
   - players - not robots
   - risks/mistakes

2. **ENTERTAINING**

   - creative
   - dramatic
   - spectacular

3. **COMPETITIVE**

   - physical challenges
   - mental toughness
   - a winning mentality

4. **SKILFUL**

   - Technical competence
   - tactical efficiency
   - team cohesion

5. **DYNAMIC**

   - athletic prowess
   - lively team movement
   - ball speed

6. **SIMPLE**

   - clear rules
   - uncomplicated tactics
   - basic language

7. **PASSIONATE**

   - intense enthusiasm
   - spirit of adventure
   - love of the game

8. **HONEST**

   - sporting behaviour
   - anticorruption
   - commitment

9. **JOYFUL**

   - fun
   - pride
   - jubilation

Photo 2

The Philosophy of a Coach

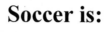

Soccer is:

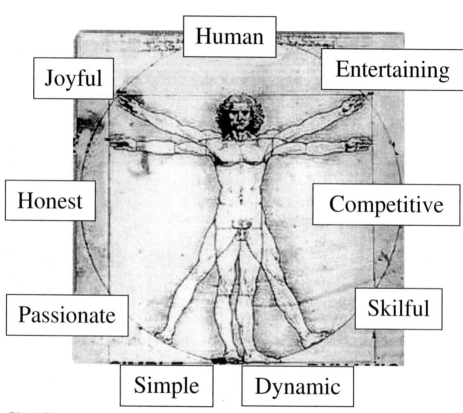

Human

Joyful

Entertaining

Honest

Competitive

Passionate

Skilful

Simple

Dynamic

Photo 3

First of all, a coach must remain calm and focused: that is, he must understand his players and team when they face critical moments. When concentration and positive tension are needed he can stave off pressure, and place the situation in perspective when the players have done their best but the result has been negative. He understands when a player needs to be helped and reassured, to be made not to feel guilty for mistakes, as this would be very dangerous from the psychological point of view.

Competitiveness is something that one learns at school and that, partly, can be cultivated and acquired: to be successful it is necessary to be competitive and have a winning mentality. Being competitive means measuring one's strength against the opposition, never being absolutely certain of being the best. It means having a good psychological balance which results in a steady drive to continuous improvement.

A good coach immediately understands the real strength of his team and combines the qualities and abilities of his players: he can tell who has more strength, intelligence, inventiveness, creativity and who is more skilled. He optimizes the individual values of his players, positioning them in the field so as to have a maximum performance "structure".

Dynamic play, speed of the ball, team movement: it is important to continuously practice the speed of the ball in passing. The exercises have a deeper meaning when they involve movement: not only passes to empty spaces for the teammate but also timely passes towards his run. During the exercises it is very easy to notice who has developed - or is endowed with - this ability: timely and quick passes to the teammates' feet in different parts of the field. At first, I get my players used to passing the ball to their teammates while counting. That is, when they control and pass, I count "1, 2, 3" and the player must have already passed the ball in a precise way towards his teammate's run. Then, when the player receives the ball he must already be in a position to make the pass in the best possible way, be it a low, precision or long pass. A slow player must receive the ball at a non-excessive speed, while a quick one at a greater speed. Only a few exercises are needed to immediately understand, both in triangulations with a third moving player and in the 30/40-yard deep pass to a running teammate, that the pass must be accurate - to the feet - and not far ahead or behind, or the sweeper or a covering opponent can stop the action. Perfection is needed and the player must be carefully coached on passes.

Today, physical conditioning is certainly more important than before: the teams win possession of the ball and counterattack so frequently all through the match and this requires the players to be fit and able to constantly perform at high level.

A coach must coach "simply" and set clear rules when he builds the team. The rules must be valid for players, coaching assistants and trainers. This simplicity can be expressed by proposing strategy, patterns and tactics based on the following principles:

- never dribble excessively;

- pass the ball as quickly as possible in depth;
- control the pace of play;
- limit risks;
- cover behind the ball;
- use tactical communication to help the teammate with the ball;
- be aware of the team's weak and strong points.

Tactics should focus on pressure to win the ball and then to quickly develop the offensive action.

A coach's passion, enthusiasm and love for soccer are vital and instrumental in determining his willingness to search for new solutions, start new initiatives, vary and differentiate the exercises that give pleasure and satisfaction to the players and the team. In this way coaching never becomes extremely repetitive. Of course, repetitions are important for learning something specific, but if they are always carried out in the same way, the players' enthusiasm can be dampened and so, in time, they can lose effectiveness.
Curiosity and a search for novelty are not to be ignored, and this applies both to players and coaches.

A sound education is based on honesty, sportsmanlike behavior and not letting others condition you. Even if sometimes an excess of competitive spirit and the determination to win might make you forget for a while the rules of sportsmanlike education, they are what you finally return to when your education is based on ethical and moral principles.

A coach must always listen to and reassure his players, be amusing and in a good mood. When he is in a bad mood, possibly due to negative results, it is important for him not to show it to the team or he could transfer it to them, with alienating results: *"come on boys, cheer up, the next time we'll have better luck..."*.
Being in a good mood, reassuring and honest has always come naturally and spontaneously to me. When I think back to Juventus, Inter Milan or Bayern Munich, where I had experiences that in Italy seemed a bit heated and not really natural..., I remember how I used to present myself afterwards to my players in a joyful, honest and warm way, with the ability to change those moods which can be extremely harmful in certain moments.

We have come back to the starting point: the human aspect. My being human, conveying feelings and vibrations from my 60 years of age and 25 years of experience, is what mostly gratifies and satisfies me. Ferri, Bergomi, Cabrini, Platini, Zickler, Strunz, Fink and many others have personally confirmed this to me.

This is to stress that if a coach is fair, consistent, spontaneous and honest, the players understand him and the team can give him what he asks of them... and all together they can obtain the maximum.

It is important, both in victories and in losses, that the coach show honesty, serenity and psychological balance, both personally as well as between himself and the teammembers. Honesty, serenity and psychological balance require open and unequivocal communication with the entire environment: managers, supporters, colleagues and mass-media. Honesty, serenity and psychological balance are vital in a much too often tense and exaggerated environment which sometimes does not respect you.

Common sense is a part of your role, your person, your being human, and a part of those moral values you have inside and which you want to convey at the threshold of the third millennium, while coaching soccer.

Finally, I think that many considerations of this philosophy apply to youth soccer too, especially those tending to help the introduction, development and improvement of the young players' technical-tactical and physical aspects, trying to structure the player's education to social and moral values, his character and his personality.

A Coach's Philosophy

Soccer is:

Human

Joyful

Entertaining

Honest

Educational Formative

Passionate

Skilful

Simple   Professional

Photo 4

"How shall we finish this book, Sir?"
"Let's finish it by saying that in soccer, at any level, the movement of the legs is always determined by the brain and the heart".